Harper College Library
3 2158 00477 9417

W9-AGZ-885

DIGITAL TECHNOLOGIES IN HIGHER EDUCATION: SWEEPING EXPECTATIONS AND ACTUAL EFFECTS

Digital Technologies in Higher Education: Sweeping Expectations and Actual Effects

Sarah Guri-Rosenblit

Nova Science Publishers, Inc.
New York

For permission to use material from this book please contact us:
Telephone 631-231-7269; Fax 631-231-8175
Web Site: http://www.novapublishers.com

LIBRARY OF CONGRESS CATALOGING-IN-PUBLICATION DATA

ISBN: 978-1-60692-238-5

Guri-Rosenblit, Sarah.

Digital technologies in higher education : sweeping expectations and actual effects / Sarah Guri-Rosenblit.

p. cm.

ISBN 978-1-60692-238-5 (hardcover)

1. Education, Higher--Computer-assisted instruction. 2. Education, Higher--Effect of technological innovations on. I. Title.

LB2395.7.G87 2009

378.1'734--dc22

2008037250

Published by Nova Science Publishers, Inc. New York

CONTENTS

Preface **vii**

Acknowledgements **xi**

Chapter 1 The Tower of Babel Syndrome **1**
Confusing Terminology *1*
'E-Learning' and 'Distance Education': Not the Same Thing *6*

Chapter 2 A New Paradigm in Learning/Teaching Practices? **15**
Sweeping Expectations *15*
Academic Faculty: Traditional Roles Throughout History *17*
Academic Faculty in the Digital Era: New Roles and Challenging Demands *20*
Principles of Good Practice in University Teaching as Benchmarks *30*
Revolution or Evolution? *36*

Chapter 3 Some Erroneous Assumptions **47**
Space and Time as Barriers to Overcome *47*
The Urge to Broaden Access *50*
Self-Evident Advantages of the New Technologies *52*
Natural Study Inclinations of Young Students *54*
Imparting Information Versus Constructing Knowledge *58*
Making Profits and Achieving Economies-of-Scale *62*

Chapter 4	Diverse Higher Education Environments	**69**
	Developing and Developed Countries	*69*
	National Academic Cultures and Policies	*78*
	Academic Versus Business Cultures	*85*
	Different-Type Institutions	*89*
	Diverse Subject-Matters	*96*
Chapter 5	Navigating between Contrasting Trends	**101**
	Globalization Versus National Needs	*102*
	Broadening Access Versus Marketization	*107*
	Competition Versus Collaboration	*113*
	Intellectual Property Versus Intellectual Philanthropy	*117*
Chapter 6	Quo Vadis? – Some Future Trends	**123**
	Promoting Institutional Diversity	*124*
	Enhancing Flexibility	*128*
	Changing Roles of Academic Faculty	*130*
	Consolidating Research Findings on Teaching and Learning	*133*
	Gradual Change of Academic Environments	*134*
	Emergence of New Technologies	*136*
References		**139**
Index		**167**

PREFACE

Technology affects nowadays practically most activities in our life. The new digital technologies have permeated economy markets, politics, our workplaces, the ways we communicate with each other, our home activities, as well as operation of all levels of education from kindergarten to doctoral studies. The impact of the new technologies has changed the speed of production and distribution of knowledge, as evidenced by the increased publications of scientific papers and the number of patent applications. The new technologies challenge higher education institutions worldwide to redefine their student constituencies, their partners and competitors and to redesign their research infrastructures and teaching practices.

The digital technologies have also generated many conflicting claims and predictions as to the present, and mainly future, effects that Internet and World Wide Web might have on higher education environments. Some futurists tell us that the information and communication technologies have already produced an era of a 'digital tsunami' and are driving the restructuring of academe by forcing educators to realign and redesign their academic work dramatically, while many others contend that the use of technology has remained, and will remain, on the margins of the academic activities and is unlikely to change in any fundamental way the dominant campus cultures. On one hand, the emergence of the new technologies has broadened access to many new student clienteles and in such a way contributed greatly to social equity in higher education, and on the other hand, the continuous development of advanced and complex technological infrastructures widens the digital divide between developed and developing countries, and between rich and poor. Most academics have adopted eagerly the many technological capabilities provided by the Internet in their research activities, and at the same time, many professors still feel reluctant to incorporate the technologies in their teaching. The digital technologies gave rise to many new providers of higher education and increased the competition in the academic global market, and at the same time we witness a growing trend of collaborations and convergence of academic practices enhanced by the new media. The World Wide Web encouraged 'digital piracy' and led to the enactment of stringent copyright and other intellectual property laws, while concurrently has enhanced an open source movement that advocates the opening up of academic work and research to the public.

These multiple contrasting trends, and the visible gap between some sweeping expectations echoed in the 1990s as to immense impacts of the digital technologies on higher education environments and their actual implementation, are dealt in this book. The various chapters in the book provide a critical and reflective view on the implementation of the digital technologies in higher education from various perspectives, based on hundreds of comprehensive reviews, books, monographs, policy statements, articles and research reports.

Chapter 1 – This chapter deals with the 'The Tower of Babel Syndrome', a confusing language and misleading conclusions, resulting from the fact that people refer to totally different roles of the digital technologies while using the same generic terms, and vice versa - use many different terms to describe the same functions. Even a modest exploration of the growing number of articles and publications describing technology innovations in higher education settings yields a long list of hard-to-distinguish terminology of more than twenty different terms which describe the employment of the new technologies in education settings. The multiple terms reflect the lack of a standardized language in the discourse on the digital media in educational settings, as well as portray different foci in relating to their impact. Some terms focus on the 'communication' and 'interaction' functions facilitated by the technologies' abilities, while other terms refer to the whole process of learning or to the overall study environment, and so on. Chapter 1 also distinguishes between 'distance education' and 'e-learning' (or any other term describing the applications of the digital technologies in educational settings), since there is a noticeable tendency to confuse between them, though marked differences exists between these two concepts.

Chapter 2 - This chapter tackles the question whether the digital technologies have induced a new paradigm in learning/teaching practices in the academic world from various perspectives. The multiple roles of academic faculty, as they have evolved throughout history are discussed, as a background for examining the new roles and challenging demands from the academic faculty in the digital era. The overload of the new roles imposed on the academic faculty in he digital era, as well as some other factors related to the distributed teaching responsibility, time consumption and lack of incentives, lack of technological literacy and support systems, enhanced burnout patterns of faculty that use the new media intensively, and intellectual property concerns, constitute immense obstacles for the optimum utilization of the digital technologies in academic settings.

Chapter 3 - This chapter examines six erroneous assumptions that explain the gap between the sweeping expectations as to the profound effects of the information and communication technologies in the academic world and their gradual and moderate implementation in reality. The first assumption relates to the notion that the need to attend a physical campus at given times is perceived as a barrier to overcome by the majority of students in higher education institutions. The second problematic assumption has been based on the belief that most universities have an urge to extend their student clienteles, if only possible. The third erroneous assumption refers to naïve belief that the self-evident advantages of the new technologies are so clear, that most academic faculty will enthusiastically adopt them. The fourth mistaken assumption has been based on the naïve belief that the young generation that was born into the digital era will prefer by and large to study through the technological infrastructures. The fifth misconception relates to the confusion between imparting information versus constructing knowledge. The last erroneous assumption, which is dealt in this chapter, relates to the projections of generating great profits out of online ventures.

Chapter 4 – This chapter analyzes the differential impacts that the digital media have on diverse academic environments. The scale of provision and the strategies of implementation are influenced by various variables: available infrastructure needed for the utilization of the technologies, the economic wealth of the countries, governmental policies, academic cultures, institutional goals, the substantive structure of various disciplines and domains of study, etc. This chapter focuses on meaningful differences that exist in the implementation process of the new technologies between: developing and developed countries, various national academic cultures and policies, academic versus business cultures, different-type higher education institutions, and diverse subject matters

Chapter 5 - This chapter discusses the intricate and subtle interrelations between four pairs of contrasting trends which challenge higher education in general, and affect as well the implementation of the digital technologies in higher education settings: globalization versus aand intellectual property versus intellectual philanthropy. University leaders as well as policy makers of online ventures and technology initiatives have to navigate nowadays between contrasting trends in defining the purpose and direction of their operation.

Chapter 6 – The final chapter sums up the most noticeable future trends that are likely to take place, following a deeper penetration of the advanced technologies into various layers of the academic world. The major trends relate to: promoting institutional diversity, enhancing flexibility, changing roles of academic faculty, consolidating research findings on teaching and learning, gradual change of academic environments, and the future development of new technologies, such as Immersive Education platforms and a growing use of mobile technologies.

This book might be of particular interest to policy makers at institutional, national and international levels of higher education, as well as for researchers and practitioners in higher education that are challenged everyday by contrasting and conflicting situations that characterize the ongoing adaptation of the new media in higher education environments.

ACKNOWLEDGEMENTS

The idea of writing a book on the implementation process of digital technologies in higher education settings grew out of a research report which I wrote in the framework of an international research team in a project which was entitled 'Higher Education in the Digital Era'. This project was conducted under the auspices of the Center for Studies in Higher Education in the University of California at Berkeley from 1999 to 2002, and it was sponsored by the Mellon Foundation. I would like to thank Dr. Diane Harley who invited me to participate in this team and headed the research project with vigor and rigor. The Center at Berkeley provided an excellent forum for the exchange of ideas between scholars from many countries. I got a research grant form the Center at Berkeley in 2002 that enabled me to spend a summer sabbatical there, and which resulted in a research report that was later published in the *Higher Education* journal on 'Eight Paradoxes in the Implementation Processes of Digital Technologies in Higher Education'. The multiple reactions which I got from all over the world first to the research report, that was published online, and later to the article, encouraged me to widen the scope of my comparative research and to further investigate the reasons that account for the wide gap between many sweeping expectations that were echoed in the 1990s as to the huge impact of the digital media in higher education and the actual reality. This broad comparative study which is based on an analysis of hundreds of wide-scope reviews, books, monographs, articles and research reports is reported in this book.

I also owe special thanks to the Rockefeller Foundation that enabled me to spend a month in the magnificent and nurturing environment at the Bellagio Conference Center in September 2005, and to the Fulbright New Century

Scholars Program, that provided me the opportunity to spend three months at the University of Maryland University College (UMUC) in 2006. These periods, made it possible to devote all my time to the consolidation of the huge literature which exists on the digital technologies into a first draft of my book. I would like to extend my special thanks to Prof. Sal Monaco, the Vice-Provost of UMUC, and to Prof. Stella Porto, the Chair of the Information and Technology Department at UMUC, who hosted me generously at their university. My stay at the US assisted me greatly in comprehending the unique features of the American higher education culture, and the unique ways in which technological innovations are adopted in American campuses.

I would like also to thank my university in many ways by enabling me to find 'extra' time to conduct this study while heading the graduate studies of Education, and by providing me with the necessary technical infrastructure and assistance.

Finally, I would like to express my wholehearted gratitude to Buma and Gideon, my husband and son - for their unlimited support, encouragement and love throughout the four years of conducting this study, for accompanying me on my voyages to the two sabbaticals at Berkeley and at Washington, and for being with in many more places which this study took me, either in person or through digital devices.

Sarah Guri-Rosenblit
Ramat- Gan
July 17th, 2008

Chapter 1

THE TOWER OF BABEL SYNDROME

CONFUSING TERMINOLOGY

The Internet is nowadays a world-embracing enterprise affecting trade, commerce, politics, communication, research and education. The new information and communication technologies have enabled to abolish national borders and institutional boundaries, and bear a tremendous potential to reshape the nature of study environments at all levels. In the last decade dozens of conferences were devoted to examining various aspects of the new technologies' impact, hundreds of scholarly articles and books were published on themes related to e-learning, and multiple new online ventures were undertaken by private and public universities, as well as by the corporate world.

The new technologies are quite complex in nature and serve a wide array of functions. They encompass many uses and are underpinned by a rich spectrum of hardware and software that can be combined in an almost infinite number of ways. Quite often the discourse on digital technologies can be characterized as suffering from 'The Tower of Babel Syndrome' - a confusing language and misleading conclusions, resulting from the fact that people refer to totally different roles while using the same generic terms, and vice versa - use many different terms to describe the same functions (Guri-Rosenblit, 2001a). In different languages, be it English, French, Spanish, Chinese or Japanese, the meanings attached to the new technologies are frequently blurred and obscure.

Part of the obscurity as to the actual and potential uses of the digital technologies in study environments is reflected in a plethora of different terms in the relevant literature trying to depict their nature. Donohue and Howe-Steiger (2005) claim that the marketplace of ideas related to the applications of the digital technologies has become a cacophony of jargon. The multiple terms reflect the lack of a standardized language in the discourse on the roles of the digital technologies in educational settings, as well as portray different foci in relating to their impact. Some terms focus on the 'communication' and 'interaction' functions facilitated by the technologies' abilities, while other terms refer to the whole process of learning or to the overall study environment.

Even the modest exploration of the growing number of articles and publications describing technology innovations in higher education settings yields a long list of hard-to-distinguish terminology. There are more than twenty terms which describe the employment of the new technologies in education, such as: Internet mediated teaching, technology-enhanced learning, web-based education, online education, computer-mediated communication (CMC), telematics environments, e-learning, virtual classrooms, I-Campus, electronic communication, information and communication technologies (ICT), cyberspace learning environments, computer-driven interactive communication, open and distance learning (ODL), distributed learning, blended courses, electronic course materials, hybrid courses, digital education, mobile learning, distributed learning, technology enhanced learning (Allen and Seaman, 2003, 2004; Anderson and Elloumi, 2004; Bates, 1999, 2005; Collis, 1995; Collis and van der Wende, 2002; Cox and Marshall, 2007; Donnelly and McSweeney, 2008; Fetterman, 1998; Gallagher, 2004; Guri-Rosenblit, 2001a; Harley, 2002; Holmberg, 1989, 2005; Jones, 2002; Khan, 1997; Kozma, 2003; Littleton and Light, 1999; Lytras et al., 2008; Mackintosh, 2006; Mena, 2007; OECD, 2005; Pfeffer, 2003; Selinger and Pearson 1999; Somekh and Davis, 1997; Strijbos et al., 2004; Tifflin and Rajasingham, 1995; Trucano, 2005, UNESCO, 2005).

Are there really important differences in meaning among all these terms and phrases? The answer is yes and no. E-learning refers to any type of learning using electronic means of any kind (TV, radio, CD-ROM, DVD, cell phone, personal organizer, Internet, etc.) (Arafeh, 2004), but in most publications it is used mainly to denote online learning through the web. 'Blended courses' indicate that there are at least two different modes of teaching and learning combined in a teaching/learning process, and 'mobile' teaching or learning puts the main emphasis on the transmission of any given content or discourse through the mobile technologies. But altogether the differences between the many terms are quite obscure.

Unquestionably, the many terms describing the uses of the new technologies in educational settings in the relevant literature reflect the ambiguity as to their roles and functions. One emphasizes the interactivity and communication functions of online communication, while another highlights the information retrieval possibilities from a wide range of remote data sources. Some are excited by the video-conferencing abilities, whereas others are focusing on the text production sophistication, the richness of multi-media packages, etc. One application can be relatively cheap (as an e-mail communication), while another possibility might be terribly costly (such as a pre-prepared multi-media program). Some abilities of the digital technologies can be used with minor alterations of the study environment, while others require a grand change and a total overhaul of the existing infrastructures.

The lack of clarity as to the meanings attached to the various terms describing the use of the digital technologies causes frequently misunderstanding of research findings and vigorous debates between researchers. For instance, Zemsky and Massy (2004a) published a controversial report on the failure of e-learning to achieve its initially proclaimed goals in American colleges and universities, entitling e-learning as a 'thwarted innovation'. One of the main criticisms raised against their report has been that they failed to define what 'e-learning' stands for.

Carol Twigg published a critique against Zemsky and Massy's report in *The Learning Market Space* entitled 'A Little Knowledge is Dangerous Thing' where she claimed that: "When I heard Bob give a talk about this study at an ECAR (*EDUCAUSE Center for Applied Research*) conference last November, my response was the same as when I read the full report: What is 'it'? ("The hard fact is that e-learning took off before people really knew how to use it"). Is 'it' a faculty member at Foothill College using PowerPoint? A company like UNext trying to attract venture capital? A distance learning program serving off-campus students? An Ivy League university setting an ivy.com? Well, the answer is clear, it's all of the above and more" (Twigg, 2004).

Twigg continues her attack by stressing that the term 'e-learning' does not stand for itself but in relation to many entities: "What are they talking about here: e-learning, e-learning products, e-learning software, e-learning activities, e-learning courses, e-learning initiatives? All of these phrases and more are used.... It really gets interesting when we arrive at the conclusion they draw from this confusion: that e-learning has gone bust. Once again, the problem proves to be definitional" (ibid).

Boume et al. (2005) from the Sloan Foundation state in their review of Zemsky and Massy's report that: "In our view the report is billed as concerning e-learning, but in actuality is concerned much more with the use of technology in teaching and learning in higher education...Claiming that e-learning has failed, the report fails to define what e-learning is".

These were just two examples of confusion as to the meaning of the generic term 'e-learning' as it appears in one specific report. Such ambiguity relates also to many more terms describing the applications of digital technologies in educational settings, in general, and in higher education contexts, in particular. The term 'virtual' is confusing no less than 'e-learning'. Pfeffer indicates that the popular expression 'virtual university' is widely used for a vast variety of phenomena. Some use this label for institutions that merely put their course catalogues online, some for universities that offer online materials for traditional courses or even a few online courses within otherwise traditional curricula. In other cases, the term is used for web-based umbrella organizations that cover online activities of some higher education institutions, for alternative providers of higher education, or even for organizations that merely act as brokers for online courses or curricula. Pfeffer claims that "this variety of phenomena to which the term is applied results in a confusing picture of what a virtual university might be" (Pfeffer, 2003, p. 2).

Part of the confusion, as to the uses of the new technologies, stems from the fact that they are complex and exhibit a wide range of qualities and abilities in different domains of educational practices. The new technologies have opened up possibilities to design new study environments that were not feasible beforehand - for both on-campus and off-campus students. Their capacities go far beyond the ability to transfer content of textbooks and lectures to students at a distance, and to facilitate the interaction between students and teachers. The digital technologies offer a real challenge and potential to supplement existing technologies and to provide new exciting possibilities to enrich and improve the quality of the study process, and to affect the delivery, production and administrative mechanisms of academic systems.

Pfeffer (2003) claims that the discourse on the digital technologies is commonly used with a strong bias towards learning/teaching processes, often reducing e-learning to web-based education, while simultaneously neglecting other activities of traditional research universities, which go far beyond the classroom interaction. The new technologies affect many other domains beyond facilitating the communication between students and teachers and in-between students. They can: alter the production process of study books and academic journals by advanced electronic publishing devices; enrich dramatically the information retrieval possibilities for both students and researchers; enhance the creation of strong research networks; change the administrative procedures and control of marketing, enrollment, loans approval, etc.; reshape the testing and examinations practices; and change the overall physical infrastructure of academic environments (Guri-Rosenblit, 2001a, 2005a). Clearly, the multiple functions and complexity of the new technologies create a confusing effect when discussed in generic terms.

Furthermore, the digital technologies change rapidly and turn their implementation in educational settings most challenging and complex. Arafeh in a comprehensive report of SRI International on the applications of the electronic technologies for distance education states that: "Technology has been moving so rapidly that it is difficult to know what to expect next, let alone what practical and policy contexts it will require. New electronic and wireless technologies and delivery systems are changing how information is conceived, packaged and transmitted...Technology is moving so quickly that trying to keep abreast of the wave from a planning and policy perspective is challenging. The future will be an increasingly complex space in which success will consist of embodying and addressing such complexity gracefully" (Arafeh, 2004, p.6).

There is also a noticeable tendency to confuse between 'distance education' and 'e-learning'. Particularly in the USA 'distance education' is defined mainly as conducted through digital technologies. A comprehensive report issued by The Pew Learning and Technology Program in the USA stated clearly that: "The terms 'distance learning', 'distance education', 'distributed learning' and 'online learning' are used more or less interchangeably" (Twigg, 2001, p. 4). Also Allen and Seaman (2003, 2004) in the extensive Sloan reports on the quality and extent of online education in the USA view online education as the main medium for distance education, though they acknowledge in the introduction of their reports that these two terms are not necessarily synonymous. Mackintosh (2006) in describing alternative models of implementing the digital technologies in higher education uses the term 'distance education technologies' as a synonym to the term 'information and communication technologies (ICT)', and so does Beaudoin (2006a,b) in his extensive book on examining *Perspectives on Higher Education in the Digital Age.*

The researchers of a comprehensive report of SRI International on *The Implications of Information and Communications Technologies for Distance Education: Looking Toward the Future* state from the outset that: "Although correspondence, telephone, television, and teleconferencing have all been effective delivery methods for distance education, the Internet has been a particularly important development in making it possible for teachers and students to access a wealth of information and each other quickly, easily and interactively in both face-to-face and remote educational settings" (Arafeh, 2004, pp. 5, 1). Therefore the SRI researchers decided to survey only distance education activities using information and communication technologies in traditional public and private institutions. However, the SRI researchers acknowledge that e-learning or virtual learning do not comprise necessarily distance education: "Virtual learning refers to immersive or simulated learning scenarios where the learner participates as an actor. These educational forms can be utilized for learning at a distance but are not necessarily synonymous with it… Many web-based activities are seen as complements to real-time or face-to-face activities in the regular classrooms" (ibid, p. 1).

Since there is a common confusion between 'distance education' and 'e-learning' (or any other term describing the applications of the digital technologies in educational settings), two meaningful differences between 'distance education' and 'e-learning' are discussed below.

'E-Learning' and 'Distance Education': Not the Same Thing

As aforementioned, many policy makers, scholars and practitioners in higher education tend to use the terms 'distance education' and 'e-learning' interchangeably as synonyms, emphasizing the continuous blurring of boundaries between conventional and distance education (American Federation of Teachers, 2000, 2001; Allen and Seaman, 2003, 2004; Arnold,

1999; Bates, 2005; Beaudoin, 2006a,b; Evans and Nation, 2000; Lewis et al., 1999; Mackintosh, 2006; OECD, 2005; Ryan, 2002; Selinger and Pearson, 1999; Trucano, 2005; Twigg, 2001).

But there are significant differences between 'distance education' and 'e-learning'. Distance education at university level has existed since the early half of the nineteenth century (Bell and Tight, 1993). The idea of a distance teaching university adopts the opposite course of a campus-based university. Instead of assembling students from dispersed locations in one place, it reaches out to students wherever they live or wish to study (Guri-Rosenblit, 1999a). E-learning, on the other hand, is a relatively new phenomenon and relates to the use of electronic media for a variety of learning purposes that range from supplementary functions in conventional classrooms to full substitution of the face-to-face meetings by online encounters.

Furthermore, distance education in most higher education systems today is not delivered through the new electronic media, and vice versa: e-learning in most universities and colleges all over the world is not used for distance education purposes (Bates 2001, 2005; Boezerooij, 2006; Collis and Moonen 2001; Gourley, 2008; Guri-Rosenblit 2005a,b; Harley et al., 2002; Mena, 2007; OECD, 2005; Pfeffer, 2003; van der Wende 2002; Vest, 2007). 'Distance education' and 'e-learning' do overlap in some cases, but are by no means identical. Though most students use nowadays various forms of e-learning, according to a survey conducted in 2001 in the USA, for example, only 7.6% of undergraduate students in the academic year of 1999/2000 took some distance teaching courses, and only 2.2% of them studied their whole degree program through distance education (US Department of Education, 2002). Douglass who summed up the state of art in relation to online education in US higher education until 2005 highlighted the fact that although 97% of US public higher education institutions offer at least one online or blended course, and 49% offer an online degree program, only 3.2% among all US higher education students took all of their courses online (Douglass, 2005).

When the new digital technologies have emerged, many scholars in the field of distance education have related to them as the new generation of distance education (Bates, 1999, 2005; Beaudoin, 2006b; Garrison, 1993, 1999; Nipper, 1989; Peters, 2001). Already in 1989 Soren Nipper in his classic analysis identified three generations of distance education: the first was correspondence teaching; the second was multi-media teaching - integrating the use of print with broadcast media, cassettes and to some degree computers; and the third generation was identified with the new interactive communication technologies (Nipper, 1989).

Below are examined two distinctive differences between 'distance education' and 'e-learning' in relation to remoteness and proximity between the learner and teacher in the study process, and the composition of the relevant target populations.

On Remoteness and Proximity

'Distance education', by its very definition, denotes the physical separation of the learner from the instructor, at least at certain stages of the learning process. This applies to distance education at all levels, from kindergarten to higher education. Holmberg, one of the leading researchers in the field of distance education, defined 'distance education' as characterized by non-contiguous communication, meaning that the learner and teacher are separated not only in space but also in time. According to Holmberg, the term 'distance education' covers "the various forms of study at all levels which are not under the continuous, immediate supervision of tutors present with their students at lecture rooms or on the same premises" (Holmberg, 1989, p. 3). But contiguous education and pure distance education are extremes that rarely exist. Many distance education providers use face-to-face tutorials, summer schools and laboratory sessions, whereas many conventional universities utilize independent study and guided learning by tutors and a variety of media. The advent of the new interactive communication technologies enables synchronous communication between students and teachers and among students from a distance.

Daniel's (1990) interpretation of the term 'distance education' embraces all forms of instruction in which classroom sessions are not the primary means of education. Distance education is mostly homework, with occasional work in class; whereas conventional education is mostly classwork with occasional work at home. In conventional education the teachers teach; in distance education the institution teaches. Keegan (1986) defined the quasi-permanent separation of the teacher and the learner throughout the length of the learning process, as well as the quasi-permanent absence of a learning group throughout the length of the learning process, as two of the major characteristics of distance education. In other words, in 'distance education' students are usually taught as individuals, not in groups, and are separated physically from both the teacher and other fellow students. In some cases, groups of students are taught by a distant teacher, mainly in the framework of teleconferencing and other broadcasting media.

Bates (2005) highlights the critical importance of technology in enabling distance education. He argues that 'distance education' is more a method of delivery and less an educational philosophy. Distance education enables students to study in their own time, at the place of their choice and without face-to-face contact of a teacher. Technological devices, from the print technology through radio, audio-cassettes, compact disc players, television and video to the current Web-based learning, have always shaped the nature of interaction between students-teachers and the taught content in distance education settings.

Although the new technologies facilitate the provision of distance education, and as mentioned earlier are also defined by many as 'distance learning technologies' (Arnold, 1999; Garrison, 1993, 1999; Garrison and Anderson, 2000; Guri-Rosenblit, 2005a; Peters 2001), 'distance' is not a defining characteristic of e-learning. The applications of electronic media in distance teaching settings constitute only partial and limited functions, out of their overall capabilities. In fact, none of the digital technologies' uses denotes the physical separation of the learner from the teacher at any stage of the study process. As aforementioned, many of the new technologies' qualities can be used most efficiently to enrich and support lectures, seminar meetings and face-to-face tutorials (Bates, 2005; Collis and Moonen, 2001; Fetterman, 1998; Guri-Rosenblit, 2002, 2005a,b; Harasim et al., 1995; Harley et al. 2002; Kurtz, 2008; Littleton and Knight, 1999; OECD, 2005; Robinson and Guernsey, 1999; Scott et al., 2002; van der Wende 2002).

OECD has conducted in 2004/5 an in-depth survey of e-learning practices in 19 tertiary education institutions in 13 countries in the Asia-Pacific region (Australia, Japan, New Zealand, Thailand), Europe (France, Germany, Spain, Switzerland, the United Kingdom), Latin America (Mexico, Brazil) and North America (Canada, the Unites States). In this comprehensive study 'e-learning' was defined as "the use of information and communications technology (ICT) to enhance and/or support learning in tertiary education. While keeping a presided interest in more advanced applications, e-learning refers to both wholly online provision and campus-based or other distance-based provision supplemented with ICT in some way. The supplementary model encompasses activities ranging from the most basic use of ICT (e.g. use of PCs for word processing of assignments) through the more advanced adoption (e.g. specialist disciplinary software, handheld devices, learning management systems, adaptive hypermedia, artificial intelligence devices, simulations, etc.)" (OECD, 2005, p. 11).

The OECD research team has defined a typology of five stages of online utilization ranging from none or trivial online presence to fully online courses. In-between these two polar ends they defined three typical stages: Web-supplemented (course outline and lecture notes online, use of e-mail, links to external online resources); Web-dependent (students are required to use the Internet for key 'active' elements of the program); Mixed mode (students are required to participate in online activities as part of the course work, which replace part of the face-to-face teaching/learning, but still significant campus attendance remains). One of the main conclusions of the OECD study is that: "Consistent with their current activities, institutions' dominant rationales for e-learning strategies at campus-based institutions centered on on-campus enhancement through increased flexibility of delivery and enhanced pedagogy" (OECD, 2005, p.13). In other words, most higher education institutions use the digital technologies to enhance classroom encounters rather than adopt a distance education pedagogy.

The digital technologies are applied in higher education institutions in teaching/learning processes for a variety of purposes: information retrieval from periodicals, books, newspapers and other information resources; simulations and multi-media presentations; communication with instructors in- and after classes; communication amongst students; drilling exercises and sample tests; reading notice boards; class administration, etc. Furthermore, the information and communication technologies have a huge impact on other important areas of university activities, such as: library management; registration and loan administration; enhancement of research communities; academic publishing; mobility and cooperation between institutions. The applications of the technologies in the above mentioned areas have nothing in common with the traditional roles of distance education.

In early 2000 the National Academies of the USA launched a study on the implications of the information technologies for the future of the nation's research universities (National Research Council, 2002). The panel was composed of leaders drawn from industry, higher education and foundations with expertise in the areas of information technologies, the research universities, and public policy. The members of the panel purported to examine the implications of the new technologies on the activities of teaching, research, service and outreach of the research university, as well as on its organization, management, and impact on the broader higher education enterprise. They concluded that the impact of the information technologies on the research university will likely be profound, rapid and discontinuous. The new technologies will not only influence the intellectual activities of the university (learning, teaching and research) but also change how the university is organized, financed, and governed. Nevertheless, they emphasized that the campus, as a geographically concentrated community of scholars and a center of culture, will continue to play a central role. In other words, the impact of the new technologies on the universities' operation and on the ways knowledge is generated and transformed will grow in the future, but most of their applications will take place in the framework of campus-based universities and not in distance or virtual settings.

Target Populations

A second distinctive characteristic of distance education is its attention to the needs of special clienteles that for a variety of reasons cannot attend a face-to-face gathering, a school or a conventional campus. Examples of intensive exchanges of letters for educational purposes have been known since ancient times. Such is the correspondence between Plato and Cicero and their students, and the famous letters sent by Apostle Paul to the early Christian communities (Guri-Rosenblit, 1999a). Since the nineteenth century correspondence institutions, extensions and distance teaching universities have opened the gates of academia to diverse clienteles for higher and continuing education. By doing so, the distance teaching institutions fulfilled an emancipatory ethos (Morrison, 1992), a kind of barrier-removal mission. Time, space, prior level of education, social class, working and family obligations were defined as barriers to be overturned by special policies and mechanisms applied by distance education institutes.

The target populations studying through distance education at post-secondary level were considered as distinct and special, usually older than the age cohorts at classical universities, and mostly 'second chance' students according to a variety of criteria. Such was the case of Prof. Knight of St. Andrews University, the oldest Scottish university, who decided that women were also entitled to higher education. He had initiated in 1877 an external higher education degree in arts specifically designed for women scattered in over one hundred centers world-wide (Bell and Tight, 1993). This program lasted until 1931. Traditionally, distance education at university level purported to overcome barriers and difficulties of students that were unable to attend a conventional campus. The obstacles which distance education has enabled to overcome include lack of formal entry qualifications; physical/health constraints; geographical barriers; working; family obligations; being held in closed institutions, such as prisons and hospitals, etc.

Interestingly, even nowadays when millions of people use the Internet and exploit its distance learning capacities, the profile of the students studying all or most of their higher education programs through distance education methods still resembles the profile of the traditional distance student (Douglass, 2005; Guri-Rosenblit, 2005a; OECD, 2005). In a comprehensive survey published by the US Department of Education in November 2002 on *A Profile of Participation in Distance Education 1999-2000*, it was clearly found that students who chose to take distance education programs were "those with family responsibilities and limited time. They were more likely to be enrolled in school part time and to be working full time while enrolled" (US Department of Education 2002, pp. iii-iv). This survey was conducted on all undergraduate and graduate students enrolled in USA post-secondary institutions during the 1999/2000 academic year.

According to a study by the American Association of University Women (2001), women are increasingly pursuing online education from a distance because of the flexibility of time it allows. In a comprehensive study conducted by SRI International in 2004, the researchers state that: "Distance education has filled always a demographic niche. Distance education students have typically been non-traditional students - those who are older, employed, married or with children, and living in circumstances such as far-off rural or unsafe urban areas that make it difficult for them to physically attend and educational institution" (Arafeh, 2004, p. 2). Some claim that nowadays some universities have relegated the special treatment of distant students in favour of providing online activities for on-campus students, ignoring the unique characteristics and needs of the students choosing to undertake higher education studies from a distance (Bates, 2007; Bullen, 2005; Bullen and Janes, 2006).

Unlike distance education, e-learning is used by all types of students in all educational levels, from kindergarten to doctoral studies. E-learning offers attractive uses for learners of all ages and of various interests and needs. Younger pupils enjoy its multi-media games and fun activities in acquiring very basic literacy skills; older students use its endless information resources for preparing homework, assignments and examinations; and millions of people use e-mail, chat groups and other formats of telecommunication as learners, and in their social and working lives. E-learning is by no way exclusively meant for distance learners. As argued earlier, it is used extensively by on-campus students in the framework of their activities in classes, seminars, laboratories and other academic assignments and projects.

In this book we relate to the use of the new technologies in both campus and distance education settings. Whenever possible we indicate the context (distance settings or on-campus applications) and the relevant domain in which the impact of the digital technologies was investigated and discussed (learning/teaching, research, administration etc.). However, quite frequently it is difficult to derive from many studies and reviews what had been the exact technological applications that they had examined. Bates had analyzed more than 200 studies on the applications of digital technologies, and attested that often it was impossible to depict from the studies what was exactly entitled as 'online learning', ' web-based learning', 'enhanced- technology teaching', etc. (Bates, 2007). In the next chapter we focus mainly on the implementation of the digital technologies in teaching/learning practices, and try to answer the grand question whether the new technologies have introduced a paradigm shift in academic teaching and learning, as some zealous proponents of the new technologies claimed a few years ago.

Chapter 2

A NEW PARADIGM IN LEARNING/TEACHING PRACTICES?

SWEEPING EXPECTATIONS

A few years ago, many economic analysts, policy makers and practitioners projected that dramatic changes would take place in the academic world. The total restructuring of learning/teaching practices in campus universities and the emergence of new-type higher education institutions were among the most sweeping predictions as to the impact of the digital technologies on higher education systems. Drucker, who is considered as one of the most important management thinkers of our time, predicted in 1997 that "thirty years from now the big university campuses will be relics. Universities won't survive" (Drucker, 1997). Several years on, the euphoria surrounding high technology industries and their sweeping effects on training markets and higher education has subsided.

Most of the far-reaching expectations were directed to the domain of learning/teaching practices. There has been a widespread belief that the use of electronic technologies would force a change in how university students are taught. It was assumed that the new technologies will transform teaching and learning processes from being highly teacher-dominated to student-centered, and that this transformation will result in increased learning gains for students, creating and allowing for opportunities for learners to develop their creativity, problem-solving abilities, information reasoning skills, communication skills, and other higher order thinking skills. Harasim et al. already in 1995 claimed that the Web-based learning represents a true 'paradigm shift' in education (Harasim et al., 1995). Laurillard (2002) in her widely acclaimed book on *Rethinking University Teaching* emphasized the pressing need of higher education institutions, both campus-based and distance education providers, to meet the demands of the knowledge society by taking full advantage of the rich possibilities which the new technologies present to move teaching and learning into a new era. In the preface to his book on *Perspectives on Higher Education in the Digital Age* Beaudoin stated that: "The rapid proliferation of digital technologies, especially within the last twenty years, is having a dramatic influence on the academy and on the conventional ways in which faculty teach and students learn" (Beaudoin, 2006a, p. vii).

Zemsky and Massy argued that the potential of the personal computers "sparked a utopian vision in which teachers taught and students learned in fundamentally different ways. Just over the horizon was a world of active learners with teachers who guided and facilitated rather than proclaimed and judged" (Zemsky and Massy, 2004a, p. 7). However, as Trucano concluded in a wide study on the applications of the digital technologies in education settings worldwide, there are currently very limited, unequivocally compelling data to support the belief that fundamental changes took place in teaching/learning practices (Trucano, 2005). Trucano's conclusions are supported by many other studies and comprehensive reviews (Ayers, 2005; Bates, 2001, 2005; Boezerooij, 2006; Boezerooy et al., 2002; Cuban, 2001; Garret and Jokivirta, 2004; Garret and Verbik, 2004; Gigling, 2004; Guri-Rosenblit, 2005b; Mackintosh, 2006; Matkin, 2002; Mena, 2007; Middlehurst, 2000, 2003; OECD, 2005; Ryan, 2002; van der Wende, 2001, 2002; Zemsky and Massy, 2004a, b, 2005; Zhang et. al, 2004).

The digital technologies have penetrated higher education in various domains, but less often than predicted have they changed the pedagogic fundamentals of the learning/teaching practices. The new technologies have greatly affected other important domains that were little referred to in the discourse on the role of technologies in higher education, domains such as - academic administration and management, libraries' organization, research networks, initiation of new fields of study and training, the physical infrastructure of the study environments, etc. Eventually, all these domains affect directly or indirectly the study process in academic settings, but in more complex and subtle ways than predicted in the early 1990s.

In this chapter we tackle the question whether the digital technologies have induced a new paradigm in learning/teaching practices in the academic world from various perspectives. It seems that the overload of the new roles, which professors are expected to undertake while using the new technologies in their teaching, constitutes a possible obstacle for the optimum utilization of the digital technologies in academic settings. Thus, we start with analyzing the multiple roles of academic faculty as they have evolved throughout history. We follow with discussing the new roles and challenging demands from the academic faculty in the digital era. Further on, we analyze the potential of the new technologies in university teaching using the Seven Principles of Good Practice in University Teaching, that were defined by Art Chickering and Zelda Gamson in 1987 (Chickering and Gamson, 1987), as benchmarks for effective and efficient teaching at university level. Last, we discuss on the basis of the multiple studies and findings related to the various applications of the digital technologies in higher education whether they have introduced a new paradigm in learning/teaching practices.

ACADEMIC FACULTY: TRADITIONAL ROLES THROUGHOUT HISTORY

The nature of the interrelations between students and academic faculty reflect the ethos and functional roles of different-type universities at various locations and throughout historical evolutions and developments. Marked differences existed even between the very first universities. The University of Bologna, that was established in 1088 and is regarded as the first university in Europe, was organized on the initiative of students who were mature, wealthy men, and who hired masters to teach subjects which they, the students, were interested in. The Italian universities from their early age tended to emphasize the practical professions, such as law, medicine, and theology (Ross, 1976; Rothblatt, 1997). The universities of Oxford, Cambridge and Paris, on the other hand, were dominated by doctors of theology, clergymen called to service, who taught what soon became known as the seven liberal arts (*Septem Artes Liberales*). Here the masters took the initiative in organizing the academic curricula and defining the students' roles. Their view of what should be taught and what should be done in the university dominated.

In England, at the center of university life was the small college and a shared domestic life of student and teacher. The attitude of the university was both paternalistic and authoritarian on one hand, and strongly individualized and student-centered on the other hand. The student was conceived as a ward of the university which was responsible for guiding his development. The idea of *in loco parentis*, by which the university assumed responsibility as the parents' substitute for the care, discipline and full education of each student, was dominant. The tutorial, the regular face-to-face meeting of student and tutor to explore and discuss the lessons and topics of the day, characterized the learning/teaching process (Guri-Rosenblit, 1999a). In the Oxbridge tradition, the tutors were, and to this date still are, responsible for examining the needs of the individual students, suggesting the tutorials and the seminars which they should attend and advising on reading lists and the whole pattern of study towards a degree. Tutors' care was not confined to academic studies only. They also gave advice on how to live as an undergraduate in the environment of the college, how to get over the psychological stress of examinations, and how to prepare for a future career. Such relationships often evolved into personal individual relationships between tutors and students well beyond the strictly academic development of the student (Rothblatt, 1997, 2007; Sewart, 1992; Bell and Tight, 1993).

Until the nineteenth century it was generally assumed in most universities that there should be a close relationship between professor and student. In the early nineteenth century the idea of the Humboldtian German university gave impetus to a new conception of student-professor relationship. The concept of *Lernfreiheit* emphasized the freedom of the student to choose his own program of study, live independently of the university, and move from one university to another, following his academic interests. The concept of *Lehrfreiheit* highlighted the freedom of the professor to investigate whatever he chose to focus on and to teach the results of his research irrespective of utilitarian applications and without government influence. This was a different type of university, with students following their own academic inclinations and way of life, and professors focusing greatly on research. The university had no obligation or intention to be responsible for the overall education of its students. The idea of the Humboldtian university has had a profound influence on shaping universities all over the world, and particularly the research-oriented universities.

Evidently, the opening up of higher education in the twentieth century, especially after the Second World War, had an immediate impact on the student-academic faculty relationship. We live in a world in which many of the long-standing assumptions about the nature of the face-to-face interaction in university settings are no longer tenable. Larger classes and a redefinition of the teachers' professional responsibilities made the intimate relations between students and their tutors or professors unrealistic, except at the most wealthiest universities or colleges which could maintain a low student-faculty ratio.

The move from the one-to-one tutorial or the small seminar group to lecture groups of dozens and even hundreds of students has led to wholly different forms of learning and teaching. Most of the undergraduate students nowadays attend many of their lectures in large auditoria, follow a series of courses taught by specialists, and the overall learning process is highly modularized and depersonalized. Mass higher education moved into a kind of industrialized mode in which the teaching process is divided among a wide range of specialists. Sewart argued that mass higher education has created "an assembly line approach in which the product representing studentship is assembled by a number of specialists, many in narrow academic disciplines, but some also in supporter areas which are at least as critical to the attainment of the final objective of successful completion of undergraduate studies" (Sewart, 1992, p. 235).

However, professors as well as adjunct faculty members in conventional universities, specializing in any field of expertise, are usually fully responsible for all of the components that are involved in teaching a course on any given subject, from its initial inception and design, through its actual teaching in the classroom or auditorium, to the evaluation of the students' achievements. At the most, the professors might be assisted by one or several teaching assistants in large classes, mainly for checking assignments and exercises. In distance teaching universities, as well as in many online teaching frameworks, this full responsibility of teaching is divided between several actors, who do not merely assist the professor in specific areas, but take over fully some of the teaching responsibilities in the development, actual teaching and assessment stages. Distance education as well as online teaching has taken the industrialized process of mass higher education a further step down the road (Guri-Rosenblit, 2004; Mackintosh, 2006; Peters, 1994, 2001, 2004).

We have focused our discussion on the interrelations between professors and students. But it is important to bear in mind that in addition to teaching, professors have many additional responsibilities. Most of them are expected to be productive scholars engaged in research of some significance. The administration of the university requires the professors to take part in the committee work of their departments and carry their share of administrative work. The professional associations, to which they belong, expect professors to show interest, participate in their activities and adhere to their standards. The community and society expect the professors to make their expertise available when it is required (Guri-Rosenblit, 2004). The use of technologies adds on additional roles, which many academics feel reluctant to undertake for a variety of reasons, which are discussed below.

ACADEMIC FACULTY IN THE DIGITAL ERA: NEW ROLES AND CHALLENGING DEMANDS

Employing the new technologies efficiently and effectively adds on additional responsibilities, beyond and *in lieu* of the traditional roles of professors, specified in the previous section. Face-to-face instruction in the classroom is familiar, effective, and well understood. Many academics feel wary about changing a well-tested paradigm of teaching (Donohue and Howe-Steiger, 2005). Adoption of the new technologies is perceived by many teachers as a risky, if not an intimidating change, and therefore quite often faculty members in many higher education institutions are not keen on participating in online initiatives (Abel, 2005; Boezerooy et al., 2002; Guri-Rosenblit, 2004; Kurtz, 2008; Massy and Zemsky, 2004a,b; OECD, 2005; Trucano, 2005). In the comprehensive OECD study on the applications of the new technologies in tertiary education institutions in 13 countries, one of the major conclusions was that: "While faculty resistance can partially be imputed to (at least perceived) pedagogic limitations of e-learning and insufficient maturity of the tools, it can also be explained by a lack of time (or motivation) to carry out what is foremost an additional task, by insufficient ICT literacy, or insufficient pedagogic literacy related to e-learning" (OECD, 2005, p. 16). Below are discussed the major demanding challenges which academic faculty are facing in the process of implementing the digital technologies in their teaching.

Distributed Teaching Responsibility

One of the challenging demands facing academic faculty nowadays, is the 'unbundling' of their professional work into discrete tasks undertaken by an array of academic, technical and administrative staff (Anglin and Morrison, 2000; Bauder, 2006; Bullen and Janes, 2006; Dede, 1995; Guri-Rosenblit, 2004; Kanuka et al., 2008; Paulson, 2002; Vrasidas and Glass, 2002; Williams, 2003). According to Schlusmans et al. (2004) the organizational approaches of a classroom-based teaching are closely aligned with artisan or craftsman practices where the academics are responsible for the entire development and delivery process of their courses. In comprehensive online teaching frameworks, as well as in large-scale distance teaching universities, the academics are required either to assume new roles or to collaborate in a team framework with tutors, editors, instructional designers, television producers, computer experts, graphic production personnel, etc. in developing and delivering their courses.

The distributed teaching responsibility, with its standardization aspects, conflicts with the long-standing culture of academics, based on autonomy in teaching and a reward system focused mainly on research (Bauder, 2006; Donohue and Howe-Steiger, 2005; Guri-Rosenblit, 2004; OECD, 2005). Clearly, in a team framework, the professors' academic freedom in teaching is reduced in comparison to their being responsible for designing the overall learning/teaching process.

When the large distance teaching universities were established in Europe in the early 1970s, Peters, the founding president of FernUniversität in Germany, argued that academics in the new distance teaching universities form a new species of professors, and that the traditional roles of professors have been challenged drastically: "It is a difficult task to switching from oral teaching to teaching by means of the written word and by merging traditional teaching techniques and modern technological ways of communication...The result is revolutionary in the sense that an academic teaching tradition of several hundred years had to be changed radically at once" (Peters, 1997, p.71).

Peters was also the first to focus on the division of labour, inherent in large-scale distance education frameworks, as a basic ingredient of his industrialization theory (Peters, 1994, 2001). He highlighted mainly the impact of the division of labour on the planning of courses, the management and administrative organization, and the control measures of teaching large quantities of students. He emphasized the mechanisms of assembly line, mass production, standardization, objectification, concentration and centralization, typical of the development of self-study materials and of the monitoring of students' learning in distance education settings. Peters related also to the differential functions of academics teaching at a distance *vis-a-vis* university teachers in conventional universities, a differentiation which derives from breaking up the complete work process of teaching into discrete functions.

Distributed teaching responsibility characterizes also many online ventures within campus-based universities. In a dual-mode university like the University of British Columbia, a typical course team includes a tenured professor; a course developer, combining project management and instructional design skills; a technology expert; an editor; a graphic designer (Bates, 2005). The professors work with all other members of the team in designing and developing their courses, and continue working with other professionals in the actual teaching - tutors, evaluation experts and technology support personnel. Such working conditions differ immensely from the sole and overall responsibility of professors of their courses which has characterized the academic teaching for over 900 years. Professors who view the academic freedom in teaching as a sacred value of their profession, resist strongly the unbundling of their teaching responsibility and the participation in a team framework (Guri-Rosenblit, 2004).

Time Consumption and Lack of Incentives

An additional important reason explaining the reluctance of many academics to engage in online instruction relates to the fact that to design study programs for online teaching constitutes a complicated and demanding task (Bates, 2005; Guri-Rosenblit, 2004, 2005b; Kanuka et al., 2008). Teaching online, or even preparing some materials for online teaching, requires faculty to devote much more time to the preparation of study materials than they would for a face-to-face classroom presentation, both if they are required to operate within a team framework or undertake the overall design and teaching of their courses by themselves. Many studies highlight the fact that academic faculty find that teaching online is time consuming, is more isolated and requires specialized skills (Arafeh, 2004; Hislop and Ellis, 2004;

OECD, 2005; Paulson, 2002; Trucano, 2005; Zemsky and Massy, 2004a,b). Even the use of the most simple e-mail function turns sometimes to be threatening for many academics. Potentially, teachers are expected to be attentive to students' queries and remarks with no time limits. Many professors view such reality as a severe penetration of their social and private life. In some studies it was found that professors decided to close their e-mails to students, since they felt that it 'vandalizes' their social and private lives (Guri-Rosenblit, 2005b). Interestingly, not only teachers, but also students indicate sometimes that online or blended courses increase significantly their workload and study time (Aycock et al., 2002; Hong, 2008).

Many professors teaching mainly online from afar feel isolated and not well-equipped to handle the multiple tasks expected from them in online teaching without a professional or collegial support. Fouche (2006) emphasized that online distance teaching turns to be an isolating experience for many tele-instructors, even more than for students who are usually connected to their peer group through chats and other support mechanisms in an online group. Fouche compared the isolation feeling as being placed in a "multi-island situation without the ocean", and strongly recommended to establish support networks for professors teaching through the digital technologies. Fouche found in his research that feelings of isolation can be significantly decreased when there is a regular contact and collaboration amongst colleagues.

Many studies specify a long list of roles which teachers are expected to undertake when utilizing the new technologies in their teaching. For instance, according to Wilson et al. (2004), instructors teaching online are expected to: Provide infrastructure for learning (syllabus, calendar, communication tools, and instructional resources); model effective participation, collaboration and learning strategies; monitor and assess learning and provide feedback, remediation, and grades; troubleshoot and resolve instructional, interpersonal, and technical problems; and create a learning community in which learners feel safe and connected and believe their contributions are valid.

Abel claims that in online learning, faculty are asked to make the biggest changes, with unclear rewards (Abel, 2005). Zemsky and Massy (2004a) indicated that many of the participating institutions in their study began to discover that they constantly had to make extra incentives available to faculty in order to involve them in e-learning. When the expenditures of those funds became too expensive, the institutions dropped the incentive programs and witnessed a general flattering of e-learning adoptions and experiments.

In a wide range study conducted by Boezerooy et al. (2002), 693 respondents from 174 institutions in seven countries (the Netherlands, Germany, UK, US, Australia, Norway and Finland) were asked, among other things, to evaluate the implementation process of the digital technologies in academic teaching. The main research question was focused on the scenarios that are emerging with respect to the use of the digital technologies in higher education. Within this context the researchers were interested in the way in which higher education institutions perceive the changes in their environment and whether and how this influences their strategic choice in respect to the use of technologies. Furthermore, they looked at how policies in relation to the integration of the new technologies are implemented and to what changes they lead in the actual teaching and learning practice and in the way instructors perceive their role. The study was conducted in 2001/2, and the expectations related to what is likely to happen in 2005 and beyond.

The study of Boezerooy et al. applied a multi-level and multi-actor approach, addressing the various actors active at various levels within the higher education institutions (decision makers, instructors, and support staff). One of the major conclusions of this study was that overall most instructors felt that they devote much time to the technology with no particular reward. Throughout the responses, the differences between respondents from different countries on this issue were found to be minimal. Interestingly, significant gaps were identified between the attitudes of policy makers and teachers in relation to the impact of the new technologies. Consistently in the study of Boezerooy et al., professors were found to be less interested and less impressed about the potential of the electronic technologies than those in the position of institutional decision making and even the support staff. Most of the professors have not actually changed their ways of teaching even though they used the digital technologies in different ways. Most teachers have indicated that there are little or no systematic rewards to devote more efforts to incorporate the technologies in their teaching. This finding is supported by many other comprehensive reviews and studies (Arafeh, 2004; Bates, 2005; Bradburn, 2002; CHEPS, 2002; Collis and van der Wende, 2002; Kurtz, 2008; Nachmias, 2002; Oblinger et al., 2001; Ryan, 2002; Trucano, 2005; Zemsky and Massy, 2004a,b).

In addition, Boezerooy et al. found in their comprehensive study that the competence of faculty to use the new technologies played only a modest role in institutions' staffing policy and that consequently the necessary incentives and reward for staff that use the technologies extensively are lacking. Since there were few policy incentives in existence in most studied institutions, most respondents did not expect there to be much change in the future (Boezerooy et al., 2002).

Lack of Technological Literacy and Support Systems

Trucano (2005) found in his encompassing review that teachers most commonly use the new technologies for administrative tasks, such as record keeping, lesson plan development, information presentation, basic information searches on the Internet, but overall are less competent in using the technologies compared to their students. Students use the new technologies in much more sophisticated ways than teachers. Many professors report that they do not feel confident in utilizing the advanced technologies. Trucano concluded that the limited confidence of many teachers using the new technologies affects the way in which the learning/teaching processes are conducted.

Trucano stressed the burning need to develop incentives in order to promote effective teacher participation in continuing professional development. Of particular note is that ongoing and just-in-time support have been recognized as crucial training and support mechanisms for the use of technology in instructional delivery (Abel, 2005; Arafeh, 2004; Brindley et al., 2004; Carlson, 2002; Fouche, 2006; Kanuka et al., 2008; Tait and Mills, 2003). Also in the OECD study it was found that all of the participating institutions acknowledged the need to recruit a broader range of staff to complement academic staff, such as technologists, instructional designers, learning scientists, etc., in order to implement the technologies more effectively (OECD, 2005).

The study of Abel (2005) purported to provide insights into best practices for achieving success in online learning. It pulled from the experiences of 21 institutions across the Carnegie classifications in the US. The 21 institutions included - five community colleges, seven BA/Master's institutions (five private, two public), and nine research doctoral institutions (one private, and 8 public). It included large to very small higher education institutions, such as Penn State University, which supports 62,000 students with online technology, on one hand, to Peirce College, which- while much smaller, generates 46% of its revenue from online programs, on the other hand. The most significant finding of Abel's study was that institutions that offer the entire degrees online are more successful than those that offer only a scattering of courses. The institutions which focused on putting full programs online were about four times as likely to perceive that they had achieved 'overwhelming success' as compared to institutions that focused their efforts at the individual course level. Putting full programs online, when done correctly and focused on student learning, involves teamwork within the academic department and among several units of the institution. Abel concludes that: "For online program to succeed, it must be thought through carefully and perhaps reengineered to serve students differently and, hopefully, better" (Abel, 2005, p. 76).

The most common success factors of those institutions implementing the 'programmatic approach' in the study of Abel included: Special support resources dedicated to the selected programs; new course and program formats to reflect the unique pedagogy of implementing the digital technologies into the various programs; program design sessions to help faculty leaders create an effective program. Institutions that adopted an overall policy of using the new technologies were doing a lot more than just posting course notes or syllabi online. However, many institutions which participated in Abel's study were still unclear about how the new technologies fit with their mission, and have found that achieving widespread adoption by the faculty is difficult. They have also found it challenging to achieve faculty use that truly enhances the learning interaction between faculty and students as opposed to simply posting materials online.

Burnout

The overload put on professors who teach extensively online has been found in several recent studies to result in a higher burnout rate as compared to professors that do not teach online (Hislop and Ellis, 2004; Hogan and McKnight, 2007; Lackritz, 2004)). Some faculty feel that the process of acquiring the knowledge and training to deliver effective online instruction and the actual teaching online constitutes a source of added stress and burnout. Burnout is defined as both a psychological and physical response to workplace stress. Pines (1993) indicated that burnout symptoms include usually fatigue, poor self-esteem, inability to concentrate on a subject or work activities. Maslach and Leiter (1997) identified six major influences on burnout: (1) workload; (2) lack of control over establishing and following day-to-day priorities; (3) insufficient reward and the accompanying feeling of continually having to do more for less; (4) the feeling of isolation in a community in which relationships become impersonal and teamwork is undermined; (5) the absence of fairness, in which trust, openness and respect are not present; and (6) conflicting values, in which choices that are made by management often conflict with their mission and core values.

Research on burnout related to higher education faculty is sparse. Lackritz (2004) examined burnout among 265 higher education faculty members and found that burnout shows significant correlations with numbers of students taught, time invested in various activities, and numerical student evaluations. Furthermore, female faculty members displayed significantly higher mean scores than their male counterparts on the emotional exhaustion scale of the MBI-ES (Maslach Burnout Inventory Educator Survey). The Maslach Burnout Inventory-Educators Survey (Maslach et al., 1996) was used to collect data from the respondents. Maslach and his colleagues identified three burnout dimensions: (1) emotional exhaustion - feeling of being emotionally overextended and exhausted by one's work; (2) depersonalization - a feeling of impersonal response toward students; and (3) a reduced sense of personal accomplishment - a loss of personal self-efficacy. According to Maslach et al. (1996) the MBI-ES is designed as a diagnostic tool to label individuals as 'burned out'. The instrument is widely accepted among researchers and addresses the three dimensions of burnout, specified above.

Hislop and Ellis (2004) found that teaching online becomes a major workplace stressor leading to burnout symptoms. Shea et al. (2006) indicated that students studying online report higher levels of learning and teaching effectiveness in situations when they perceive higher levels of teaching presence, such as active directed facilitation and effective instructional design practices. One way for online instructors to be effective is to be online constantly, which leads quite often to burnout (Dunlap, 2005).

In a study conducted by Hogan and McKnight (2007) burnout has been identified as a significant factor among those in instructional positions using the digital technologies. In this study 76 online instructors teaching at the undergraduate level within US universities were interviewed. The 76 university instructors who participated in Hogan and McKnight study were teaching courses in a technology-enhanced format. Data analysis revealed that online instructors possessed an average score on the emotional exhaustion subscale, high degree of depersonalization, and low degree of personal accomplishment. The final conclusion of Hogan and McKnight was that the online instructors were on the borderline of burnout showing signs of moving toward a high degree of burnout.

Some researchers emphasize mainly the isolation feelings of professors teaching online as the main reason for decreased job satisfaction and alienation from the institution in which they are employed (Fouche, 2006; Kanuka et al., 2008). Particularly new academics, experience a sense of isolation that eventually progresses toward "exasperation, disillusionment, and eventual alienation" (Kanuka et al., 2008, p. 161). Kanuka et al., claim that appropriate support systems that enhance continuing learning opportunities for the academic staff teaching online, without having opportunities to meet colleagues on a campus, might reduce feelings of isolation and provide social and professional support.

Wood and McCarthy (2004) emphasize that it is far better to prevent burnout before it develops. They offer several measures, such as to: Discuss with academic faculty who teach online issues that have an impact on shaping the study environment; provide appropriate support mechanisms; describe in detail expectations from the faculty in order to reduce role ambiguity and uncertainty; create and maintain clear lines of communication between faculty teaching online and administrators by giving performance feedback; provide mentoring and advanced training for online teaching; and most important - reduce teaching load and number of students per online courses. The last recommendation is particularly problematic, since small numbers in online classes result naturally in higher costs, which undermines one of the main raison d'être of engaging in online teaching. The cost issue will be discussed in detail in the next chapter.

Intellectual Property Rights

Concerns about intellectual property rights may also be seen as a barrier for the implementation of e-learning in academic environments. For instance, in a conference which convened in October 2003 in Cambridge Mass., the network for Academic Renewal of the American Association of Colleges and Universities attempted to explore the interrelations between 'Technology, Learning and Intellectual Development', and focused particularly on the key issue - why such a low percentage of the faculty use digital, online and other technologies in teaching and learning, when compared with the eagerness of the same faculty seized upon these technologies for research, writing and publication (Abel, 2005). One of the major questions in this conference related to intellectual property. Faculty members were worried whether they are going to lose intellectual property over their course materials if they make even a portion of their materials available online. It seems of tremendous importance to clarify ownership of usage rights of intellectual property generated by and for teaching.

There is a different perspective related to copyright. If rules of copyright become too stringent, and faculty will not be able to refer easily to other works in online settings, as they do regularly in classroom teaching, it might deter them from utilizing the new technologies in their teaching. Michael Tanner, a professor of computer science in the School of Engineering at the University of California in Santa Cruz, emphasized in his testimony before the Representatives of the US Copyright Office that: "My experience as both a member of the faculty and an administrator persuades me unequivocally that faculty will not participate in developing the potential of the Internet for teaching if they cannot easily adapt what they now do in the classroom to the new medium. Tremendous creative effort goes into developing digital enhancements for classroom and independent student learning...Within the physical classroom, the educational exemptions have allowed faculty to focus all of this effort on intellectual and pedagogical issues. If the networked environment requires complex, time-consuming, and uncertain negotiation for permissions, or if faculty feel constantly anxious about infringing copyright, they will turn their attention in safer directions. Innovation will be stifled" (Tanner, 1999). Tanner's main argument was to expand the existing copyright law's exemptions for education, to include also online teaching.

The issue of copyright and intellectual property rights is a hot topic discussed in multiple books and research publications (Dowd, 2006; Dupin-Bryant, 2006; Gantz and Rochester, 2005; Lindsey, 2003). Public policy and relevant legislation are gradually developing in this domain to protect individual rights. The intricate interrelations between the conflicting trends of preserving intellectual property, on one hand, and promoting intellectual philanthropy through the 'open source' movement, on the other hand, are elaborated in Chapter 5.

PRINCIPLES OF GOOD PRACTICE IN UNIVERSITY TEACHING AS BENCHMARKS

The Seven Principles of Good Practice in Undergraduate Education were developed in the US by convening a group of scholars of higher education that were asked to derive from their knowledge of the past 50 years of research a set of principles that could be applied to improve learning. It was supported by the Board of the American Association for Higher Education (AAHE). The Principles were created by Art Chickering and Zelda Gamson with help from higher education colleagues, AAHE and the Education Commission of the States, with support from the Johnson Foundation. The AAHE Bulletin first published the Seven Principles of Good Practice in Undergraduate Education in March 1987 (Chickering and Gamson, 1987). With support from Lilly Endowment that document was followed by a Seven Principles Faculty Inventory and an Institutional Inventory and by a Student Inventory (Chickering and Gamson, 1991). The principles and the inventories were widely disseminated to academic faculty in US campuses, as well as in Canada, the UK and other countries. The Seven Principles are the best known summary of what decades of educational research indicates are the kinds of teaching/learning activities most likely to improve learning outcomes. They constitute a meta-analysis of 50 years of research on good teaching principles that apply to teaching and learning in higher education environments.

The Seven Principles have been since their publication a guiding light for evaluating quality university education, and they represent a philosophy of engagement, cooperation, learning community, interaction, quality, and efficiency (Graham et al., 2001; Hong, 2008; Puzziferro-Schnitzer, 2005). They are an excellent rubric to assess the quality of teaching practices, policies and overall effectiveness. As such we choose them as benchmarks to examine the potential and actual impacts of the digital technologies in learning/teaching processes in higher education. The Seven Principles are:

- Good practice encourages student-faculty contact.
- Good practice encourages cooperation among students.
- Good practice encourages active learning.
- Good practice gives prompt feedback.
- Good practice emphasizes time on task.
- Good practice communicates high expectations.
- Good practice respects diverse talents and ways of learning.

Obviously there are numerous ways to use the digital technologies to implement the Seven Principles in university teaching. However, the compelling questions are:

- To what extent do the new technologies enable to implement effectively the Seven Principles?
- To what extent do the new technologies possess the potential to improve student outcomes and the quality of the learning/teaching processes?

1. Good Practice Encourages Student-Faculty Contact

Chickering and Gamson (1987) stated that frequent student-faculty contact in and out of class is a most important factor in student motivation and involvement. Faculty concern helps students get through rough times and keep on working. It also enhances students' intellectual commitment and encourages them to think about their own values and plans.

Unquestionably, electronic mail, computer conferencing, and the World Wide Web increase opportunities for students and faculty to converse and exchange work much more speedily than before, both in campus-based institutions, and even more so in distant settings (Chikering and Ehrman, 1996). The new communication technologies have the potential to increase the connectivity to faculty members, help them share useful resources, and provide for joint problem solving and shared learning. Ehrman (2002) stressed that the digital technologies can strengthen faculty interactions with all students, but especially with shy students who are reluctant to ask questions or challenge the teacher directly. It is often easier to discuss values and personal concerns in writing than orally, since inadvertent or ambiguous nonverbal signals are not so dominant. The literature is full of stories of students from different cultures opening up in and out of class when email became available.

Nowadays, the asynchronous communication enables to communicate with teachers after classes much more easily and frequently than ever before. The potential for an enhanced communication between students and teachers exists, but the biggest problem is whether all teachers are willing to be accessible all day long to interact with their students. As discussed earlier, some teachers feel reluctant to open their e-mails with no time limitations at all, and feel that their private and social lives are sometimes severely invaded (Guri-Rosenblit, 2004; Harley et al., 2002).

2. Good Practice Encourages Cooperation Among Students

Chickering and Gamson (1987) indicated that learning is enhanced when it is more like a team effort than a solo race. Good learning, like good work, is collaborative and social, not competitive and isolated. Working with others often increases involvement in learning. Sharing one's ideas and responding to others' improves thinking and deepens understanding.

Quite clearly, the increased opportunities for interaction with faculty discussed above apply equally to communication with peer-students. A clear advantage of electronic mail is that it opens up communication among classmates even when they are not physically together. Collaborative study groups, chat rooms, discussion boards for assignments, have the potential to enhance group work and communication among students in any study process. Unquestionably, the digital technologies have intensified collaboration between students as compared to traditional interaction in classrooms, and as such have contributed markedly to the enhancement of the second principle in the Seven Principles.

3. Good Practice Encourages Active Learning

Chickering and Gamson (1987) stated that learning is not a spectator sport. Students do not learn much just sitting in classes listening to teachers, memorizing prepackaged assignments, and spitting out answers. They must talk about what they are learning, write reflectively about it, relate it to past experiences, and apply it to their daily lives. They must make what they learn part of themselves.

The third principle follows clearly the underlying philosophy of the constructivist psychology, which will be discussed further on in Chapter 3. Knowledge is constructed actively through interaction either with others or with prior experience and knowledge. There is a wide range of the new technologies that encourage active learning. E-mail, chat groups and discussion boards enable students to reflect on studied themes and respond to each other's reflections. There are many tools for learning by doing, such as simulations, virtual reality programs, etc. Thus, it can be concluded that the digital technologies enable and enhance the third principle of the Seven Principles.

4. Good Practice Gives Prompt Feedback

Chickering and Gamson (1987) stated that knowing what you know and don't know focuses your learning. In getting started, students need help in assessing their existing knowledge and competence. Then, in classes, students need frequent opportunities to perform and receive feedback on their performance. At various points during college, and at its end, students need chances to reflect on what they have learned, what they still need to know, and how they might assess themselves.

Feedback and evaluation are most important in any study process. There are multiple ways in which the new technologies can provide feedback. In the very basic drill and practice programs, computers record and analyze personal and professional performances, and provide immediate feedback. In the framework of portfolio evaluation, computers can provide rich storage and easy access to student products and performances. Computers can keep track of early efforts, so instructors and students can see the extent to which later efforts demonstrate gains in knowledge, competence, or other valued outcomes (Chickering and Ehrman, 1996; Ehrman, 2002). Hence, it can be concluded that the digital technologies provide a range of tools to enhance ongoing feedback in the learning/teaching process.

5. Good Practice Emphasizes Time on Task

Chickering and Gamson (1987) claimed that time plus energy equals learning. Learning to use one's time well is critical for students and professionals alike. Allocating realistic amounts of time means effective learning for students and effective teaching for faculty.

Ehrman (2002) indicates that the new technologies can improve time on task for students and faculty alike by using tools like the calendar and time-reminders as one way to keep students' time on-task. Time efficiency particularly increases when interactions between teacher and students, and among students, fit busy work and home schedules. Enabling students to access remote data sources and to communicate with teachers and peer students from home or from work or from any preferred study environment, can save hours otherwise spent commuting to and from campus, finding parking places, and so on.

On the other hand, as aforementioned, many studies also indicate that working with the new technologies is frequently time consuming, most particularly for teachers, and this constitutes an acute problem which explains part of the reluctance of many faculty members to utilize the digital technologies more intensively in their teaching practices.

6. Good Practice Communicates High Expectations

Chickering and Gamson (1987) proclaimed that when one expects more, one will get it. High expectations are important for everyone - for the poorly prepared, for those unwilling to exert themselves, and for the bright and well motivated. Expecting students to perform well becomes a self-fulfilling prophecy.

Through the digital technologies teachers can communicate high expectations explicitly and efficiently. Some faculty report that students feel stimulated by knowing their finished work will be "published" on the World

Wide Web (Ehrman, 2002). With technology, criteria for evaluating products and performances can be more clearly articulated by the teacher, or generated collaboratively with students. General criteria can be illustrated with samples of excellent, average, mediocre, and faulty performance. These samples can be shared and modified easily. They provide a basis for peer evaluation, so learning teams can help everyone succeed. However, it does not seem that the new technologies have a unique advantage over traditional ways of communicating high expectations.

7. Good Practice Respects Diverse Talents and Ways of Learning

Chickering and Gamson (1987) stated that many roads lead to learning. Different students bring different talents and styles to college. Brilliant students in a seminar might be all thumbs in a lab or studio; students rich in hands-on experience may not do so well with theory. Students need opportunities to show their talents and learn in ways that work for them. Then they can be pushed to learn in new ways that do not come so easily.

The new technologies can provide different methods of learning to heterogeneous students clienteles, and accommodate various learning styles. They can offer more feedback for slower students and more challenging tasks for able students.

In sum, it can be concluded that the digital technologies have the potential to both enable the implementation of the Seven Principles of Good Practice in university teaching, and even enhance and strengthen the application of some principles. However, it is important to stress, that there is a huge gap between the potential of the technologies and their real application. Some uses of the new technologies are quite promising but require substantial reorganization and rethinking of the faculty roles, and some of the uses require major changes in the organization of individual courses or even a whole overhaul of the institutional infrastructure. Although some of the technological applications which enhance the Seven Principles have succeeded and have made impressive changes in higher learning, too many others have flowered briefly and withered, or never flowered at all. Often, the very technology that helped spark interest in some applications was blamed some years later as inadequate, and accused as the main reason for the innovation's failure (Ehrman, 2002).

Unquestionably, teachers constitute the most important factor in enabling the use of technologies to promote the Seven Principles of Good Practice in Teaching (Hong, 2008). Trucano (2005) concluded in a wide survey of technological applications in education that both in developed and developing countries teachers remain central to the learning process. A shift in the role of teachers utilizing the new technologies does not obviate the need for teachers to serve as leaders in the classroom. Traditional teacher leadership skills and practices are still important. The incorporation of the technologies in teaching does not transform teacher practices in and of itself (Cuban, 2001). Teachers' pedagogical practices and reasoning influence their uses of the technologies. Without providing adequate infrastructures and support systems for academic faculty to utilize the wide applications of the technologies, the gap between the potential of the technologies and the reality will remain wide and profound. As aforementioned, the new technologies require the academic faculty to assume new roles and tackle many challenging demands. Institutional policies need to give high priority to user-friendly hardware, software, communication platforms and ongoing support systems in order to help the technologies' potential to be materialized.

REVOLUTION OR EVOLUTION?

An innovation is judged to be radical when it challenges the underlying premises of the prevalent practice in any given field and has the potential to deliver dramatically better performance or outcomes. As Zemsky and Massy stress, in the beginning, it is the new technology's promise rather than its performance that attracts initial adherents. A large part of the promise is the vision of an altered future - one that is not different, but also dramatically better (Zemsky and Massy, 2004a).

The compelling question in our context is: *To what extent have the new technologies induced radical and pervasive change in teaching and learning in higher education settings?*

Zealous advocates of the new technologies claim that indeed the electronic technologies have introduced a radical shift in teaching. The fact is, that already in some universities, e-learning provides not just a supplement to traditional teaching, but an alternative or parallel pedagogy (Adkins, 2002; Ashby, 2002; Barajas, 2003; Clark, 2001; Donnelly and McSweeney, 2008;

EDUCAUSE Center for Applied Research, 2006; Gallagher and Newman, 2002; Gladieux and Swail, 1999; Harper et al., 2000; Hiltz et al., 2001; Peters, 2004). On the other hand, many others state that the implementation of the new technologies in academic teaching is rather evolutionary. Multiple studies and wide-range surveys and reports point to the fact that the electronic technologies so far have added mainly additional functions to the existing practices and enriched the learning/teaching processes, but by no way have they challenged the fundamental practices of teaching and learning in education, in general, and in higher education, in particular. Although student take-up of some online courses is growing steadily (Allen and Seaman, 2003, 2004; American Federation of Teachers, 2000, 2001; Bradburn, 2002; Cox and Marshall, 2007; Cox et al., 2004; Curran, 2001, 2004; George, 2005; Green, 2001; OECD, 2005; UNESCO, 2005; US Department of Education, 2002), at most campus-based institutions enrolments in online activities are relatively low and represent a small share of total enrolments. Below we present major findings of wide-range studies and reviews related to the supplementary functions of the digital technologies, impacts on student achievements and the effects of institutional policies on the implementation of the technologies.

Add-on Functions

One of the major problems in the implementation process of the new technologies in higher education is that they mainly have added new dimensions to the study process that were not existent before, but have not replaced most of the learning/teaching practices both in campus and distance education institutions. In the Israeli Open University, for example, most of its over 600 courses have a web home page and they use various aspects of online dimensions. In most of these courses - the new technologies have neither replaced the study materials, nor have they substituted the tutorial meetings. The online dimensions of the courses incorporate: chat groups, multi-media experimental kits, home pages with updated materials, administrative functions of class management, video-conferencing, etc. All of these functions replace just partially the existing ingredients of the learning/teaching process (Guterman et al., 2008). No doubt, that the add-on functions of the information and communication technologies are enriching the study experience, but at the same time are costly when offered in addition to the expensive process of developing self-study materials in distance teaching universities rather than replacing them.

As a matter of fact, most of the online courses in successful distance teaching universities are based on existing textbooks and materials, which the students are either receiving through mail or asked to purchase them on their own, as is the case in the University of Maryland University College (UMUC), the most successful public distance teaching university in the USA (Guri-Rosenblit, 2001b, 2005a).

Also, in campus-based universities, the new technologies are used mainly for add-on functions and not for substituting face-to-face encounters. The fact that the new technologies are used mainly to enhance on-campus learning, without substituting either the teacher or the classroom is well recognized in many studies (Bates, 2005; Bernard et al., 2004; Garret and Jokivirta, 2004; Garret and Verbik, 2004; Guri-Rosenblit , 2005a,b; Hanna, 2003; Harley et al., 2002; Hong, 2008; Losh, 2005; Middlehurst, 2003; OECD, 2005; Pfeffer, 2003; Vest, 2001, 2007).

Many studies point out that both students and academic faculty seem to like the traditional classroom encounters, even when given the opportunity to being exempt from attending a class, and provided with all the needed materials and assignments online. Moreover, even when professors use e-learning products and devices, most of them still teach as they were taught - that is, they stand in the front a classroom providing lectures intended to supply the basic knowledge the students need (Kurtz, 2008; Nachmias, 2002; Zemsky and Massy, 2004a,b).

On the basis of examining dozens of studies on the applications of technology in higher education settings, Bates states that the digital technologies do not replace previous practices but instead complement them: "Computers are now commonly used for PowerPoint presentations to deliver lectures, and the Internet is now being used more and more to access Web sites to support lectures. Technology used this way does not replace either the teacher or the classroom. Using technology to supplement classroom teaching does not radically change teaching methods. It merely enhances what would be done in the classroom in any case" (Bates, 2001, p. 17). Hanna (2003) concludes in his study on past and future organizational models in higher education, that the new technologies have not fundamentally changed the traditional academic culture and structure. Computers help many to perform various activities more efficiently, but still have not substantially changed the essential format of pedagogical practices by most of the academic faculty in different-type higher education institutions.

A large-scale comparative study on the applications of the new technologies in 174 higher education institutions in seven countries (The Netherlands, Germany, the UK, the USA, Australia, Norway and Finland) (Collis and van der Wende, 2002) was presented at an international conference on 'The New Educational Benefits of Information and Communication (ICT) in Higher Education' that took place in Rotterdam in September 2002. The final conclusions of this study were: "Change in relation to the use of ICT has been gradual and unsystematic. Many experiments and pilot projects have been launched leading to interesting innovations, which are, however, generally not well disseminated. ICT is used mainly to increase flexibility in on-campus delivery of education. Institutions turned out to be only moderately focused on new target groups, such as lifelong learners and international students" (CHEPS, 2002, p. 2).

The study of Boezerooy et al. (2002), mentioned earlier, indicates that the use of technology, in terms of e-mail, word processing, PowerPoint, and the Web, has become standard as part of the teaching and learning process in most universities and colleges. But this has not radically affected the nature of the teaching process. Rather, the new technologies have become part of the blend of on-campus delivery. In particular, Web-based systems are seen as valuable and leading to more efficient practices. The use of e-mail, PowerPoint, word processing and Web resources, has become commonplace, but in a way that only gradually is stretching on-campus practices.

The fact that the change is slow, and not radical, is validated by another international survey of the Observatory of Borderless Education, which was carried out both in developed and developing countries (Garret and Jokivirta, 2004; Garret and Verbik, 2004). This survey was conducted with the aim to test the widespread perception during the so-called 'e-education bubble' between 1997 and early 2000 that online learning would quickly and fundamentally rupture the conventional campus-based model of higher education. The conclusion from this survey was that online learning has had only relative impact on campus and on distance education. Change has been relatively rapid as for modest online components and for institution-wide learning platforms. But a fundamental move away from on-campus provision has not been materialized.

In the wide study of Trucano (2005) it was clearly found that the new technologies are very rarely seen as central to overall learning process. Trucano concludes that: "Studies on the use of ICTs suggest that despite rhetoric that ICTs can enable new types of teaching and learning styles, for the most part they are being used to support traditional learning practices" (Trucano, 2005, p.35). This reflects the reality in both developed and developing countries.

In the comprehensive OECD study, aforementioned, it was found that provision with 'high' online presence accounted well under 5% of total enrolments at most OECD sample institutions (OECD, 2005, p. 12). Current institutional strategies do not back the assumption that tertiary institutions will gradually move their provision towards fully online delivery. The OECD and Observatory surveys clearly demonstrate that fully online provision at campus-based institutions will remain very much a minority in the short to medium term, and that e-learning is used mainly as supplementary to on-campus delivery at undergraduate level. The OECD study has highlighted the fact that skepticism about the pedagogic value of e-learning and staff development are probably the most challenging factors in the implementation of the digital technologies. In most examined institutions this factor was found to be stronger even than key barriers, such as lack of appropriate infrastructure and funding. One reason for the faculty skepticism probably lies in the fact that e-learning has not really revolutionized learning and teaching to date. Far-reaching, novel ways of teaching and learning, facilitated by the new technologies, remain nascent or still to be invented (ibid, p. 14).

The OECD study concluded that: "It is clear that for the majority of the sample institutions, fully online programs will remain very much a minority activity in the short-to-medium term. This is certainly the case for campus-based universities, which predominantly predicted the continuation of a vigorous campus-based face-to-face teaching and learning environments. No institution with a significant campus-based element predicted fully online provision greater than 10% of total programs by 2006/7. There was no pattern in terms of more or less research-intensive campus-based institutions" (ibid, p. 39). These findings are supported by many additional studies (Arafeh, 2004; Bates, 2005; Guri-Rosenblit, 2004, 2005b; Guterman et al., 2008; Harley et al., 2002; Kurtz, 2008; Mena, 2007; Nachmias, 2002; Trucano, 2005; World Bank, 2000, 2002a,b; Zemsky and Masy, 2004a,b, 2005).

Impact Studies on Students' Achievements

Some studies focus on measuring the impact of the new technologies on students' achievements. For instance, Hiltz et al. (2001) did a meta-analysis of 19 empirical studies comparing student learning and other subjective measures in asynchronous learning online (ALN) compared to traditional face-to-face learning, and found that the evidence is overwhelming that ALN tends to be as effective or more effective than traditional modes of course delivery at the university level.

Russel (2001) examined more than 200 citations of empirical research on the implementation of the digital technologies in elementary and secondary education, higher education, adult education and professional training. His major conclusion was that there is no significant difference between achievements of students who studied through educational approaches that have used technology and those that have not. What was found to really matter was a good educational content and pedagogy, and not the technology. Such comparisons lead to zero-sum results, to the 'no significant difference phenomenon'.

Clark (2001) argued that if it is the case that the amount of learning produced by different media is similar (there is no significant difference on students' achievements), and all approaches are adequate to meet our instructional goals, then all treatments are equally valuable for learning, but still differ in their cost and convenience. This fact provides policy makers and teachers the opportunity to adopt the technology that is most cost-effective, whether human- or media-based, and that suits best their pedagogical preferences and personal style of teaching.

According to Trucano (2005) the positive effect of the digital technologies in education has not been proven. In general, and despite thousands of impact studies, the effect of the new technologies on student achievements remains difficult to measure and open to much reasonable debate. A review of hundreds of studies on the impacts of new technologies on student achievements yields few conclusive statements, pro or contra, about the use of the technologies (Ponzurick et al., 2000; Rovai et al., 2006; Schramm et al., 2001; Sikora and Carroll, 2002). For every study that cites significant impact, another study finds little or no such positive impact.

Moreover, Trucano highlights the fact that many studies that find positive impacts of the information and communication technologies on student learning rely to an often uncomfortable degree on self-reported data, which may be open to a variety of possible biases. The fact is that where the impacts of the technologies are measured by most standardized tests, few such gains are found. Trucano stresses that a lot of work has to be done in the area of monitoring and evaluation. Bias is a very real issue in most of the monitoring and evaluation work done on the information and communication technologies in educational settings. Currently, there are no common international usage, performance and impact indicators for the use of technologies to improve student achievements.

Trucano provides some interesting insights as to results presented in impact studies which measure students' achievements following a technological intervention in the study process. First, 'Computer Aided Instruction' has shown to slightly improve student scores on some reading and math skills, although whether such improvements correlate to real improvements in student learning is debatable. Second, the application of the technologies yields less effective, or even ineffective, results when the goals for their use are not clear. Third, in many impact studies there seems to be a mismatch between the methods used to measure effects and the nature of the learning promoted by the specific uses of the technologies. For example, many studies tend to look only for improvements in traditional teaching and learning processes and do not look for new processes and knowledge related to the use of the technologies. And fourth, as aforementioned, specific uses of the digital technologies prove to have positive effects on student achievement when they complement a teacher's existing pedagogical philosophy.

In sum, the current state of art indicates that studies on the impacts of the technologies on students' achievements do not yield conclusive evidence that online learning is an improvement over traditional education.

Institutional Policies

Institutional policies have an important impact on the implementation of the digital theologies. It seems that policy matters greatly in enhancing the use of technologies (Boezerooij, 2006; Boezerooy et al. 2002; Collis and van der Wende, 2002; Harley, 2002; Martinez, 2004; Vest, 2007). In the previous phase of the late 1980s and early 1990s, the role of policy may have been perceived as minor in the implementation process of the new technologies, in the sense that many initiatives were driven by a handful of innovators and early adopters (Zemsky and Massy, 2004a). Nowadays, institutional policies play a crucial role in the adaptation process of the digital technologies in educational settings. As Hoffman stated, for e-learning to become a dominant learning pattern - technology alone will not suffice (Hoffmann, 2005). The main challenge for both institutions and governments is now to develop more strategic policies on how the digital technologies can be used for the different target groups that higher education is expected to serve in the knowledge economy in the 21st century. These target groups include traditional learners as well as lifelong learners from both within or outside national jurisdictions.

In the study of Collis and van der Wende (2002), aforementioned, it was found that most of the participating institutions lack a strategic view on using the advanced technologies. The lecture remains the 'core medium', the instructional form that is most highly valued. However, institutions that have a clearer view on their mission with respect to serving different target groups (e.g. lifelong learners or international students) with online teaching demonstrate higher levels of use of the technologies and wider use of the technologies in the general teaching practice. Awareness of and response to changing demand from these new target groups and a strategic commitment to being successful in these markets seems to be a major drive for change in these institutions. Collis and van der Wende state in the final conclusions that: "In general, it can be said that the outcomes of the present study were confirmed by and large by the international experts at the seminar in Rotterdam as well as from other research. As one of the experts in the seminar stated: 'The data presented fits very much some global trends of implementing the new ICT in various places', and it seems that a quite stable state of art in this field is starting to be defined" (Collis and van der Wende , 2002, p. 63).

Also in the study of Abel (2005) it was clearly demonstrated that successful institutions in online learning had compelling reasons to support such learning. Many of them stated as their mission to serve working adults coupled with the strong need of these students to have more flexibility in receiving effective instruction. In all of these institutions there was a predominant leadership style that most likely contributed to the success in achieving mission alignment. The leadership elements were: A long-term commitment to the initiative; investment of significant financial and other resources in the implementation process of the new technologies; prioritization of expenditures on high-impact programs; and a clear understanding by the academic faculty of why the institution is implementing online learning. In particular, the involvement of key leaders in prioritizing where to focus online learning development activities was critical and highly correlated with perceived success in these institutions.

The study of Boezerooy et al. (2002) indicated that overall it seems that higher education institutions do not expect any revolutionary change as a result from or related to the use of the new technologies. There is not really a concern about being forced to change by external forces or developments. Rather, a 'business as usual' approach is taken, without anticipating any real dramatic changes in mission, profile or market position. Nevertheless, institutions are gradually 'stretching the mold', they change their procedures and models as a process of change from within.

Beaudoin emphasized the importance of leadership in implementing the digital technologies: "Schools and colleges in the new millennium need leaders who have reflected on their experiences and internalized understandings about their own capacity to lead...Indecision and immobility during these tumultuous times could prove fatal to a number of institutions, and it is the presence of effective distance education leadership that could well make the difference between success and failure" (Beaudoin, 2006b, p. 10). Individual faculty operating without any training or support and without adequate resources may become disenchanted with both the product and the process, and this reaction might naturally extend to their students. Such an outcome only reinforces the innate skepticism regarding the beneficial applications of the digital technologies in academe.

In sum, it can be concluded that most of the studies to date suggest that change in the core teaching practice, if it occurs on a substantive scale, is likely to involve an evolutionary process of assimilation, rather than a sharp revolutionary change anticipated by some early observers. Bates stated in his comprehensive book on *Technology, E-Learning and Distance Education* that there is an overstatement about virtual learning constituting a paradigm shift, at least in terms of current practice. Bates concluded that: "Until we reach the point of creating unique formats and approaches to learning that cannot be replicated in the classroom, the claim that online learning is a pedagogical paradigm shift remains to be validated" (Bates, 2005, p. 147). It seems quite clear, that many forecasts that predicted the replacement of the campus university by the new technologies have not been substantiated at all in reality, and the traditional styles of learning and teaching still reign dominantly in most higher education settings, both in distance education frameworks and in campus-based institutions. The growing use of information and communication technologies in the last decade has not challenged the campus centrality in any higher education system so far.

Chapter 3

SOME ERRONEOUS ASSUMPTIONS

In this chapter we purport to explain the gap between the sweeping expectations as to the profound effects of the information and communication technologies in the academic world and their gradual and moderate implementation in reality. There are several good reasons for the piecemeal adaptation of the digital technologies in higher education settings. Many of the predictions as to the sweeping effects of the new technologies on higher education have been based on some erroneous assumptions, six of which are examined below.

SPACE AND TIME AS BARRIERS TO OVERCOME

One of the erroneous assumptions as to the fast spread of e-learning was based on the notion that the need to attend a physical campus at given times is perceived as a barrier to overcome by many students. This perception is echoed in many publications. A report issued by US National Academies of Science in 2002, for example, stated that the new technologies "will erode, and in some cases obliterate, higher education's usual constraints of space and time" (National Research Council, 2002, p. 2). In his comprehensive book on *Perspectives on Higher Education in the Digital Age* Beaudoin claims that: "We now can envision a not too distant future where the geographic hegemony of higher education will be eliminated because students simply won't need to come to a campus to learn, and where the teaching will be less critical to the very raison d'être of higher education" (Beaudoin, 2006b, p. 3).

But the fact is that most students, and particularly those of traditional college age, enjoy attending the physical campus and meeting their peers in the framework of classrooms, lecture halls and seminar rooms for reasons that go far beyond the acquisition of knowledge and skills. The need of humans to socialize is essential, not only in higher education. Alvin Toffler (1980) coined in his famous book on the *Third Wave* the term 'electronic cottage'. He predicted a return to the cottage industry on a new, higher, electronic basis, and a new emphasis on the home as the center of society. In reality, his predictions have not been materialized. Some business firms decentralized their work, and a handful of professionals like nowadays to work at home, but still most people prefer to work outside their homes, because of their immense need for social interaction. This social need applies to higher education settings as well.

Many studies in the last decade show clearly that most students prefer to attend classes even when provided with the opportunity to get video-taped lectures, exercises and intimate tutoring through the electronic media. For instance, a large scale study was conducted at UC Berkeley from September 2000 to June 2002 on the use of technology enhancement in some large undergraduate courses in chemistry (Harley et al., 2002). This study found that only 16% of the students would be willing to watch lecture webcasts entirely online instead of going to the lecture hall. 84% of the students indicated that they prefer to attend face-to-face encounters, even though they could have studied all the materials, conducted all of the experiments and watched the video-taped lectures at home.

A wide national project in Israel to enhance the use of the digital technologies in Israeli universities through special funding and incentives provided by the Israeli Council for Higher Education, was joined by many academics. A study in 2002 showed that at Tel-Aviv University more than 1,000 faculty members have utilized various forms of the new technologies in their classes, but only 1% of them used electronic media to substitute for class encounters (Guri-Rosenblit, 2002; Nachmias, 2002). Also a recent study conducted at Bar-Ilan University on the adoption of the new technologies by academic faculty showed that though 23% of the professors use in their teaching the new technologies to some extent, only 1.1% provide fully online courses (Kurtz, 2008). Most of the technology users prefer the hybrid mode. Many more studies substantiate this trend, as discussed earlier in Chapter 2 (Arafeh, 2004; Bates, 2005; Boezerooy et al., 2002; Carneavale, 2004;

CHEPS, 2002; Collis and van der Wende, 2002; Collis and Moonen, 2001; Curran, 2001; Fetterman, 1998; Green, 2001; Heyneman and Haynes, 2004; Johnson, 2001; Johnstone and Baker, 2020; Matkin, 2002; Martin and Jennings, 2002; Schell, 2004; OECD, 2005; van der Molen, 2001; van der Wende, 2002; Zemsky and Massy, 2004a, b).

Not only students in campus universities, but also students in distance teaching institutions express a high demand for personal interaction with academics and other students. One of the main lessons derived from the operation of the large-scale distance teaching universities in the last thirty years underlines the importance of social interaction in learning/teaching processes. Contrary to some initial theories which assumed that adult students choosing to study via distance education methods prefer to learn on their own and to interact only from time to time with academic staff, the experience of the large distance teaching universities has shown that many prefer frequent contact, both with academic faculty and fellow students (Guri-Rosenblit, 1999a,b; Brindley, et al., 2004; Tait and Mills, 2003). In some places, where distance does not present a real physical obstacle, like in Israel, more than 80% of the distant students urged the Israeli Open University to provide weekly meetings with their tutors in nearly 100 local study centers spread throughout the country.

At the University of Phoenix, a subsidiary of the giant Apollo Group, the largest accredited private distance teaching university in the USA that has been operating since 1976, only about 10% of its student population were registered for online programs in 2001 (Ryan, 2002). In the last years the proportion of online students has grown to 25%. In 2005, 70,000 online students were enrolled at Phoenix University out of at total of 280,000 registered (Phoenix, 2008). Nevertheless, still most of the adult students prefer to study either at class or through the blended mode. Phoenix University has operated in 2008 in 239 physical learning centers throughout the US. It offers three modes of instruction: local students who meet their teachers in the local centers, online students who study all of their program through online instruction, and the blended mode in which students combine both online and face-to-face teaching. It seems that the 'bricks and clicks' model, offering both an online and distributed face-to-face option is regarded as the best solution for the working adult market.

Also in the business world, many prefer hybrid courses. There is an apparent resistance by many students to the notion of exclusively online education. One demographic group targeted by many universities is the busy professional, unwilling to commit to weekly classes and highly mobile in work patterns. A hybrid model has emerged for professional continuing education, combining online communication/resources supporting intensive residential periods on campus to engender group cohesion and social learning. A large study conducted in several European countries found that only 15% of companies using e-learning preferred a stand-alone approach, with the majority opting for greater online interaction and use of e-learning to prepare for and reinforce face-to-face provision (Ryan, 2002).

In other words, space and time constitute barriers for those students that due to a variety of constraints cannot attend a campus or a residential school at specific times. These are the students who have traditionally been attracted to distance education, and their numbers are likely to grow in the future. But space and time do not constitute a universal problem for most students, particularly for the traditional age cohorts that attend school and undergraduate studies at a university or at a college.

The Urge to Broaden Access

A second erroneous assumption regarding the impact of the new electronic media on the academic world was based on the notion that most universities have an urge to expand their boundaries and to extend their student clienteles, if only possible. The fact is that most campus universities have no good reason to increase their student body and to utilize the new technologies in order to mobilize new student clienteles studying from a distance. In the wide-scope OECD study, which was conducted in higher education institutions located in 13 different countries, it was clearly found that most investigated universities were not eager to increase their student clienteles: "Contrary to the predictions of the dot-com boom, distance online learning have generally failed to emerge as significant activities or markets to date. This form of activity is small scale, peripheral and poorly tracked centrally. The complex possibilities of remote international activity were typically left to small scale, department-led experiments" (OECD, 2005, p. 12). This policy is echoed clearly in many wide surveys and in-depth studies conducted on the utilization of the digital technologies in higher education (Arafeh, 2004; Garret and Jokivirta, 2004; Boezerooij, 2006; Boezerooy et al.,

2002; CHEPS, 2002; Collis and van der Wende, 2002; Garret and Verbik, 2004; Martin and Jennings, 2002; Trucano, 2005).

The elite research universities, in particular, are, by their very nature, less interested in widening access to large numbers of students. They are inclined to remain selective for the few and well-to-do students. MIT is a leading institution in ICT applications. Since the early 2000s it has run more than forty projects related to various uses of the new technologies (Olsen, 2002; Vest, 2004, 2007). Nevertheless, its president (until 2004), Charles Vest, stated firmly in his 2000/1 annual report that: "The residential university will remain an essential element of our society, providing the most intense, advanced, and effective education. Machines cannot replace the magic that occurs when bright, creative young people live and learn together in the company of highly dedicated faculty" (Vest, 2001). MIT is currently developing its Open Courseware project for 'intellectual philanthropy' purposes, but not for its own students. The Open Courseware project gives interested students and faculty members all over the world a glimpse of the MIT curricula of about 1,550 courses. But by no means does MIT intend to enroll large numbers of students, or offer online courses by MIT professors for credit (Olsen, 2002).

In a large survey of the National Center for Education Statistics that was conducted in 2003, American higher education institutions were asked to rank 15 factors that were keeping them from starting or expanding their distance education courses through the new technologies. For 44% of the institutions that did not deliver any distance education courses, and also have indicated that they were not planning to offer such courses in the next three years, the major factor perceived as keeping them from starting distance education was the lack of fit with the institution's mission (National Center for Education Statistics, 2003). Many of these institutions were private four-year universities or colleges. Expanding their boundaries through offering online courses to students outside their campuses has been perceived by their leaders as contradicting their raison d'être.

In spite of the apparent difficulties to implement the digital technologies into the traditional learning/teaching practices, a growing number of universities use the digital technologies to export a variety of programs as a commodity for profit. Many new consortia have been founded in the last decade, most noticeably by American, Australian, Canadian and British universities that export professional and academic programs for international students located mainly in third world countries. These consortia purport to generate more funds for the ongoing operation of the participating universities (Adelman, 2000; Bok, 2004; Caelis International, 2004; Clark, 1998; Cohen, 2005; Douglass, 2005; Guri-Rosenblit, 2005b; Ryan, 2002; van der Wende, 2002; UNESCO, 2002, 2003). Most of the exported programs are aimed at graduate and postgraduate students, and have achieved the greatest success in professional training. This trend of higher education's marketization will be elaborated more broadly in Chapter 5.

SELF-EVIDENT ADVANTAGES OF THE NEW TECHNOLOGIES

The new electronic media were introduced into the academic world as a sudden thunderstorm without having time to define what are the purposes and functions that they can fulfill or substitute. The lack of clear problems has turned out to be an acute problem in the adaptation process of the new technologies in universities and colleges (Guri-Rosenblit, 2005a). As discussed earlier in Chapter 1, distance education at university level purported traditionally to overcome barriers and difficulties of students that were unable to attend a conventional campus for a variety of reasons. The target populations studying through distance education at higher education have been usually older than the age cohorts at classical universities, and mostly 'second chance' students according to a variety of criteria.

Unlike the clear obstacles and barriers which traditional distance teaching technologies were designed to overcome, the digital technologies have offered multiple uses with no clear relation to any existent or future problem in the teaching/learning processes in campus universities. The initial reactions of many academics asked to incorporate the new technologies into their classrooms have been of the type: 'If it ain't broken, why fix it?' or 'Technology is the answer - but what are the questions?' (Guri-Rosenblit, 2004, 2005b).

In the controversial report of Zemsky and Massy, on the implementation of the new technologies in higher education, which was presented in the previous chapters, they indicated that one of the wrong assumptions of the e-learning pioneers was that: "If we build it, they will come" (Zemsky and Massy, 2004a, p. iii). As with most innovations, those responsible for the experimentation that yields the initial product simply assumed that their customers will recognize the value of their product as soon as it emerges on the market. Almost all of e-learning's first applications began precisely that way. Zemsky and Massy claim that the entrepreneurs' enthusiasm produced too many untested products, that in their initial form turned out not to deliver as much value as promised. This is why they believe that "e-learning took off before people really knew how to use it" (ibid). The fact is that e-learning, particularly in the US, attracted a host of skilled entrepreneurs and innovators who sought, as their most immediate goal, to establish early prominence in an industry that had yet to be defined. Zemsky and Massy emphasize that in seeking that advantage, they were aided by two phenomena. First, the boom in commercial e-learning enterprises followed more than a decade of experimentation by faculty with the use of computers in teaching. A few experiments even flowered into commercially successful products such as Maple and Mathematica, applications designed to teach students calculus using electronically mediated instruction. While such work involved only a minority of faculty, they were enough to advocate the new technology and assure university leaders that the expertise needed for e-learning ventures was available. As it turned out, that experimentation proved to be too narrow to feed the e-learning boom that followed.

The dot-com boom provided a second major impetus. It spawned exaggerated estimates of the market for Internet-based services. In retrospect, the rush to e-learning produced more capacity than any rational analysis would have said was needed. The hard fact is that the implementation of the technologies into the campuses started before most of the academic faculty really knew how to use it, and for what purpose. There was clearly missing a proven knowledge base of sufficient breadth to convince the academic faculty that the adaptation of the technologies was necessary.

The new technologies boasted the potential of being design-rich, being capable of delivery anywhere and at any time, and being fully customizable to take full advantage of each individual student's personal learning style. However, as discussed in Chapter 2, the impact of the new technologies on learning and teaching is still unclear, and open to much debate. Moreover, there is frequently a disconnection between the rationales most often put forward to advance the use of new technologies in education and their actual implementation. In Chapter 2, some additional factors explaining the resistance of academic faculty to engage in online learning or to incorporate the technologies to some extent in their teaching were discussed: the unbundling of their teaching responsibility into discrete tasks shared with an array of academic, administrative and technical staff; great amounts of time consumption for preparing materials and being attentive to students queries on an ongoing basis; lack of incentives for doing additional chores and activities; lack of adequate training and technological literacy; lack of appropriate and friendly support systems; and concerns about intellectual property rights.

The study that was conducted at UC Berkeley from September 2000 to June 2002 on the use of technology enhancement in some large undergraduate courses in chemistry (Harley et al., 2002), mentioned earlier, constitutes an interesting example of the impact of problem definition on institutional decision making. In the process of conducting the study, it was found that the technology-enhanced classes in chemistry can save both faculty time and space. Instructors spent less time answering routine questions because students were able to find some of the necessary information online. And it was also found that laboratory sessions could hypothetically be reduced from four hours to three to better utilize lab space. Such findings have been most interesting for the UC Berkeley's policy makers in face of the Tidal Wave II, namely an increase of the enrollment of about 63,000 (a 43% increase) full-time students that the University of California ten-campus system has anticipated in the coming years (Douglass, 2001, 2005). If through the use of technology it is possible to save from 10% to 20% of space and faculty time, technology becomes a strategic solution to absorb more students, although it does not save money (Harley et al., 2002).

Unquestionably, the clear definition of goals and exact domains in which the digital technologies should be incorporated, might improve greatly the efficient adaptation of the technologies in various contexts in different-type higher education institutions. The clearer is the institutional vision in relation to the digital technologies, the wider is the successful and efficient usage of the technologies by the institution's academic faculty and students (Abel, 2005; Kurtz, 2008; Natrins, 2004).

Natural Study Inclinations of Young Students

Many believe that the new generation of students prefers already, and will prefer even more in the future, to study through the digital technologies (Candy, 2004; Castells, 2000; Cummings et al., 2002; Dede, 2005; Gross,

2004; Hartman et. al, 2005; Jones, 2002, 2003; Levin and Arafeh, 2002; Oblinger, 2003; Oblinger and Oblinger, 2005; Peters, 2004; Veen, 2005). Arafeh in a wide study of SRI International on the use of technology in education settings stated that one of the underlying assumptions of the study was that: “Students of today differ substantially and qualitatively from students of yesterday in many ways" (Arafeh, 2004, p. 39). Oblinger (2003) believes that in effect, we face today a new brand of students that have and need different skills. They all have different expectations of their lives, use education differently to meet their educational goals, are more technologically savvy, and take more responsibility for their personal and educational activities. These, in turn, require different educational experiences.

When asked to present his vision as to how education will look like in 2020 in the framework of EDUCA Berlin that took place in December 2005, Prof. Wim Veen stated that: “It is a generation of students that has been born with a PC mouse in their hands and a computer screen as a window to the world. I have called this generation *Homo Zappiens*. This generation has grown up with technology and learns through computer screens, icons, sound, games, exploration, and questioning; its members also show non-linear learning behavior. Traditional books, lectures, and text-based e-learning do not suit *Homo Zappiens*, who wants to be in control of its own learning process using tools that support its information processing skills" (Veen, 2005).

In contrast to the assumption that the millennial students (those born after 1982) constitute a different species of students as compared to earlier generations, other scholars believe that most of the students today use the technologies extensively for various purposes, but not necessarily for learning. Obviously, the youngsters of today have access to and use more media than students in the past, but many of them use the media mainly for playing and recreation purposes, rather than for studying. Zemsky and Massy (2004a) claim that one of the wrong assumptions as to the applications of the digital technologies in higher education was that "the kids will take to e-learning like ducks to water", but in reality it has not happened.

Most of the interviewed faculty in the study of Zemsky and Massy in 2001 thought that students would be able and willing to utilize computer-based learning as part of a course or instead of a face-to-face course. But in reality it turned to be that students used the computers mainly to be entertained by games, music and movies; and they also wanted to present themselves and show off their work in sophisticated ways festooned with charts, animations and pictures. Zemsky and Massy believe that the promoters of e-learning simply missed all of this devotion on the part of students to complex presentations of self. The students they saw in their mind's eye were gamers who would love simulations, who would see in the computer a tool for problem-solving. And, in fact, there are some students just like that. But most others - are not. Zemsky and Massy conclude that e-learning is seen by many students at its best as convenience and at its worst as a distraction (Zemsky and Massy, 2004a,b).

Furthermore, the fact the youngsters know how to play complicated games on the computers, download music and prepare sophisticated PowerPoint presentations does not turn them automatically into computer experts when it comes to learning. When Schramm et al., (2001) examined student perceptions of the effectiveness of web-based courses, they revealed that students generally felt inadequately trained for online course experience and reported lower levels of communication with both their teachers and peers, and most of them attested that they found the online method of delivery less effective and less satisfactory than on-campus courses. Some studies highlight the fact that many students find it hard to adjust to online or blended courses, and require special guidance and assistance to understand the process of studying in such courses. Utilizing the technologies efficiently requires continuous support of the students and guidance about the pace of instruction and the acculturation to online learning (Ali and Elfessi 2004; Aycock et al., 2002; Heinstorm, 2005; Ho and Burniske, 2005; Hong, 2008; Martyn, 2003; Schramm et al., 2001; Selwyn, 2003).

Ponzurick et al. (2000) in analyzing attitudes of students towards face-to-face versus distance education courses found that many students enroll in online courses primarily because of convenience, but also feel that the online learning format is less satisfying than the traditional classroom experience. Hara and Kling indicate that many students studying in online courses reported confusion, anxiety and frustration due "to the perceived lack of prompt or clear feedback from the instructor, and from ambiguous instructions on the course Web site and in e-mail messages from the instructor" (Hara and Kling, 2001, 68). Some students also expressed feelings of isolation as a stress factor in the online study process.

Sikora and Carroll (2002) while analyzing the results of the wide scope National Postsecondary Education Descriptive Analysis Report conducted by the US National Center of Education which surveyed in 1999/2000 more than 60,000 students, indicated that a sizeable number of students were found to be less satisfied with online courses than with traditional face-to-face encounters. Results were consistent when data were disaggregated by student age and by type of institution. An interesting comparative study was conducted by Rovai et al. (2006) that analyzed students' evaluation of teaching for fully online and on-campus classes of same courses delivered during a four year period and taught by the same three professors who have each received awards for teaching excellence. Interestingly, the results of this study show that students tend to evaluate online courses more negatively than on-campus courses. All these findings indicate that many students are not so enthusiastic studying online, and often feel uncomfortable and not well-prepared to enjoy the 'any time' any place' format in pursuing academic studies.

The Educational Testing Service (ETS), the non-profit group that created the SAT in the US and a number of other standardized tests, has worked since 2001 with educators, information technology experts, and other institutions to develop a new test designed to measure what it means to be literate in the digital age (ETS, 2008). In their overview, they approach higher education institutions with the following question: "Your students can text message and download music files, but can they problem solve and think critically in a digital environment?" From their experience they conclude that: "Today's students are part of a technology-savvy generation, but they are often still at loss when it comes to using their critical thinking and problem solving skills in a digital environment; a skill set identified as Information and Communication Technology (ICT) Literacy". The pilot testing of the ICT Literacy Assessment began in January 2006. The test is built around five critical components of the ICT Literacy that are defined on the ETS site: (1) Access – knowing about and knowing how to collect and/or retrieve information; (2) Manage – applying an existing organizational or classification scheme; (3) Integrate – interpreting and representing information, which involves summarizing, comparing and contrasting; (4) Evaluate – making judgments about the quality, relevance, usefulness or efficiency of information; (5) Create – generating information by adapting, applying, designing, inventing or authoring information. The design of the ICT Literacy test by the ETS demonstrates clearly that studying effectively and efficiently through the digital technologies requires training and study, and cannot be taken for granted as a natural attribute possessed by the young generation.

IMPARTING INFORMATION VERSUS CONSTRUCTING KNOWLEDGE

A fifth misconception relates to the confusion between information and knowledge. The Internet enables access to boundless information of any nature, but there is an immense difference between imparting information versus constructing knowledge. It seems that in the sweeping enthusiasm as to the endless possibilities of accessing remote data bases and resources, somehow the essential distinction between information and knowledge has been blurred and confused. The traditional role of educational establishments at all levels, from kindergarten up to university, has been to assist their students to construct knowledge through guidance, tutoring and personal attention, and not merely to impart information. Children could have studied at home from encyclopedias and books instead of going to school, if the main purpose of education was to acquire pieces of information. There is a huge difference between having a bag of flour and knowing how to transform it into bread. Accessible information does not turn automatically into meaningful knowledge without the assistance of a teacher or an expert. Novices in any educational framework, be it an elementary school or undergraduates at a university, need the ongoing support and guidance of expert teachers in the process of constructing new information into meaningful knowledge.

Arthur Clarke, one of the most celebrated science fiction authors of our time, wrote in his essay *2001 A Cyber Odyssey- Arthur Clarke's Optimistic Guide to Surviving the Information Age* that the history of communications is littered with failures of imagination and failures of nerve. Seeking information through the Internet "is rather like a parched man endeavors quench his thirst by putting his head into Niagara Falls" (Clarke, 1999). The Information Age has opened many doors for our eager minds to explore. However, we should never lose sight of the ancient truth that "quantity is the enemy of quality". Clarke stresses that it is vital to remember that "information- in the sense of raw data- is not knowledge, that knowledge is not wisdom, and that wisdom is not foresight. But information is the first essential step to all of these" (ibid).

The new technologies provide unlimited access to information of all kinds for all types of students at all educational levels. People frequently complain that they feel lost in the overload of information they get, and sophisticated search engines have been designed, and are continued to be designed, to assist in finding relevant information as fast as possible. Moreover, the digital media and interfaces encourage multitasking, which sometimes results in a cognitive overload and concomitant loss of effectiveness (Dede, 2005; Oppenheimer, 2003).

The Open Courseware Project of MIT, mentioned earlier, provides an excellent example of the inherent limitations of materials put free on the Interne (Olsen, 2002; Vest, 2007). By putting syllabi and some other relevant materials of about 1,550 courses online, MIT provides an excellent example of 'intellectual philanthropy', and as such it has led the current open source movement. But the study load which suits the profile of the MIT students does not necessarily fit students in many other higher education institutions. Already, some professors at other universities worldwide indicated that the load of the MIT courses is too heavy for their students, and the materials adequate to be studied for a quarter period at MIT will have to be studied for a whole year by the students of their institutions (Olsen, 2002). The adaptation of the materials is conducted in each setting by expert teachers. Very few, if any, independent students were and are able to benefit from the MIT materials and substitute them for registering at a teaching institute. This is particularly true at the undergraduate level.

Wagschal (1998) stressed that frequently wrong questions are asked when introducing the digital technologies into the academic world. According to Wagschal, fundamental questions should be raised regarding the kind of knowledge needed by students entering the 21st century, and the appropriate ways to achieve such knowledge. Nachmias argued that the starting point for the creation of a research agenda and an intelligent discourse on the use of the electronic media in higher education teaching should include addressing issues such as: epistemology, learning, cognition and culture, rather than opportunities and possibilities offered by the digital technologies to education (Nachmias, 2002).

There are interesting interrelations between different epistemologies about the nature of teaching, learning and knowledge, the skills needed in a knowledge-based society, and the use of available technologies. Cross (2005) claimed that conventional instruction has been based for decades on a hierarchical model in which those who know teach those who do not know. Ultimately, there are answers to every question, and scholarship consists of knowing the answer or knowing how to find it. The epistemology underlying this mode of instruction is based on the assumption that knowledge is accumulated by discovering the 'truth' about the reality that exists. It can be discovered through scientific research, stored in libraries and computers, and can be transferred from researchers to practitioners or from experts to novices.

In the last decades there has been a noticeable move towards a constructivist epistemology. Constructivism is a philosophy of learning based on the premise that knowledge is constructed by the individual through his or her interactions with the environment. It has its roots in the constructivist movement of cognitive psychology, which holds that individuals build their own understanding of the world through experience, maturation, and interaction with others (Rovai, 2004). According to the constructivist theory learners construct knowledge actively through dialogue and discussion. Many cognitive psychologists state that knowledge can be constructed personally, through reflection and relating new knowledge to prior experience, or socially, through interaction or discussion with others, such as teachers, other learners or family and friends. Either way, knowledge becomes personal and embedded within a context which is relevant to the learner's own life and experience. The constructivist theory places more emphasis on information management and analysis, knowledge construction, problem solving, and decision making rather than on comprehension and memory. From the constructivist viewpoint, the learner is an active processor of information, in sharp contrast to behaviorism, in which the learner is perceived as a passive recipient of information.

Several scholars have claimed that technologies such as the Internet appear to facilitate this kind of learning more easily that print-based technology does. Particularly, the ability to communicate over time and place with others, and the interactive nature of the digital technologies have coincided with the underlying assumptions of constructivist approaches to learning. With the communication and sharing ability provided by e-mail, chat, Web discussion forums and other interactive technologies, people are exposed to more varied and frequent interaction opportunities than humans have ever experienced before. Many publications on Web-Based learning focus on helping learners to 'construct' their own meanings of concepts and ideas presented in the course of studying various subjects (Derntel et. al, 2003;

DiSessa, 2000; Duffy and Kirkely, 2004; Giordan, 2004; Lander et al., 2004; LaPointe, 2006; Rovai, 2004, 2007; Rovai et al., 2006; Siemens, 2004; Woo and Reeves). Herrington and Oliver (2002) have claimed that educational applications of the Web can support and improve highly effective types of learner-to-learner interactions based upon social constructivist theory. Online teachers can provide, through various communication tools, guidance, coaching and feedback. Furthermore, the interactive nature of the Internet allows learners to reach a rich spectrum of resources and establish connections with a plethora of knowledge domains (Vrasidas, 2000; Vrasidas and Glass, 2002; Vrasidas and McIsaac, 1999). However, it is quite clear that meaningful interactions are unlikely to occur without the provision of an instructional design model that fosters such interactions (Woo and Reeves, 2006).

A vast literature implies that just by creating the 'right online environment' skills of constructing knowledge will be developed. Particularly, discussions and group work can contribute to the development of collaborative, participative learning environment (Harasim, 2000; Rovai, 2004; Woo and Reeves, 2006). Bates argues that these claims do not fit his wide experience in implementing technologies in education settings (Bates, 2005). He indicates that when well designed, online discussion forums can enable learners to construct their own meanings, increase their depth of understanding of key concepts and principles in a subject, and apply concepts and ideas to new concepts. It is less clear though from the literature on online knowledge construction whether learners develop new knowledge that has not been constructed and validated before. It is also dangerous to assume that knowledge construction will always lead to a better understanding of a subject area. According to Bates, students need to be aware of the epistemological requirements of a subject and ensure that their understandings are consistent with the rules for validating knowledge in each relevant subject area. Indeed, there is increasing evidence that even good online programs do not automatically lead to the development of knowledge construction in ways that are important within a particular subject domain. It follows that the intervention of expert teachers in the study process is crucially important for constructing meaningful and valid knowledge in any domain, and the teachers' role is most significant in teaching novices, such as undergraduates in higher education, both in face-to-face and distant/online settings.

Woo and Reeves highlighted the fact that though interaction is crucial for constructing knowledge, not every interaction in a Web-based learning environment does have an influence on increased learning: "Idle chatting, online surfing, or mindlessly clicking Web pages is unlikely to lead to substantive learning even though learners are interacting with other objects" (Woo and Reeves, 2006, p.18). Vrasidas and McIsaac (1999) stressed that what is needed in order to construct knowledge is not merely interaction, but a meaningful interaction. Meaningful interaction is not just sharing personal opinion. A meaningful interaction must stimulate the learners' intellectual curiosity, engage them in productive instructional activities, and directly influence their learning. The essence of a meaningful interaction holds true for both campus-based encounters and online interactions. A Web-based environment does not provide better conditions for a meaningful dialogue.

MAKING PROFITS AND ACHIEVING ECONOMIES-OF-SCALE

A sixth erroneous assumption related to the implementation of the digital technologies in higher education was based on their fast profit making capabilities. A few years ago many analysts, such as Morgan Keegan (2000), projected billion dollar e-education and e-training markets globally. Virtual networks of colleges and universities became a marker of a new economy. Globalists have assumed that the information technologies and the Internet create a platform for brand name and entrepreneurial providers to enter new markets, essentially offering courses that are economically scalable and that reap large profits (Douglass, 2005; Newman et al., 2002). During the dot-com. boom the promise of lower program development and delivery costs compared to conventional campus-based provision was one of the most frequently cited advantages of e-learning in tertiary education and beyond (OECD, 2005). Several years later costly experience has caused many higher education institutions to question the increasing costs of their commitments to digitization and wired campus programs (Allen and Seaman, 2003, 2004; Bates, 2005; Douglass, 2005; Guri-Rosenblit, 2005b; Matkin; 2002; OECD, 2005; Ryan, 2002).

Much of the promise of the new technologies to gain large profits has revolved around simplistic ideas about the nature of the higher education market and the predilections of both providers and consumers. It turned out to be that developing online coursework is frequently far much more expensive, difficult and ethereal than once expected. In some cases it has been even more costly and time-consuming for a university than traditional classroom teaching. Analyzing the cost structure of electronically mediated education, Rumble demonstrated that e-education is more costly than traditional distance education delivery and suggested "that it may prove to be more costly than traditional education" (Rumble, 2001, p. 230). E-learning requires expensive technical support, and in order to be efficient class sizes need to be smaller to compensate for the loss of classroom interaction.

Several reasons account for this misconception regarding the fast and easy profit generation from e-learning. One reason relates to the economies-of-scale provided traditionally by distance education providers. One of the major benefits of distance education at university level in the last decades has been its ability to broaden access to higher education by providing economies-of-scale. This is particularly true since the 1970s, when a new brand of large scale distance teaching universities has been established (Bernath and Hulsmann, 2004; Daniel, 1996; Guri-Rosenblit, 1999a; Hulsmann, 2004; Potashnik and Adkins, 1996).

The mega distance teaching universities followed the model of the UK Open University that was founded in 1969. There are about thirty such universities in various parts of the world. All of these large scale universities were a product of governmental planning set to fulfill national missions, mainly - to absorb large numbers of students at a lower cost as compared to traditional campus universities (Daniel, 1996). This goal has been achieved through an industrialist model of operation, discussed earlier in Chapter 2 (Peters, 1994, 2001). The division of labor of the academic teaching responsibility into two separate phases constitutes the essence of the industrial model of distance education. The first phase is devoted to the production of high quality self study materials. The second phase consists of the actual teaching of large numbers of students by lower rank academic faculty. As the number of students increases, the cost per student decreases. Some of the large distance teaching universities teach dozens of thousands of students.

It seems that the economies-of-scale provided by the large distance teaching universities, operating on the basis of the industrial model, led many to believe that any distance teaching technology is by its very nature cost effective. As indicated in the OECD study (2005) many of the e-learning supporters argued that lower costs would result from increased automation of development and delivery processes of course materials. But given that the major impacts of e-learning have been on-campus where the technologies are mainly used as a supplement to classroom activities rather than substitute the face-to- face interaction, such cost savings have not taken place. Even online applications for administrative purposes seem to typically complement rather than substitute for traditional procedures - also undermining significant cost reductions.

In addition to the misunderstanding as to the essential difference between the industrial mode of distance education and e-learning, two additional factors account for the misconception as to the fast and easy profit making from implementing the new technologies in higher education settings. One factor relates to the substantial cuts of training costs that took place in the corporate world as a result from cuts of flights and hotel expenses on training. The other factor relates to miscalculating the costs of utilizing the new technologies by setting up an appropriate infrastructure, and creating support systems for ongoing maintenance, as well as for wastage management.

The cuts of costs in the business world caused many to assume that such money saving will occur also at universities employing e-learning (Guri-Rosenblit, 2004; 2005a,b; OECD, 2005). Obviously, it is more economical to bring training programs to the work place rather than sponsor the sending of workers for days to remote conference sites and training sessions. It is no wonder then that most of the profit making claims have come from the business and corporate world (Keegan, 2000; Matkin, 2002; Newman et. al., 2002). But cuts in hotel and flight expenses have no relevance at all for students and faculty in the academic world.

Plenty of ventures had been initiated in providing online learning by universities and the business world. Side by side with some successful collaborations, many joined ventures between leading universities and giant corporations failed to yield the initial expected results. Many business models for online programs were predicated on booming employer demand, without establishing end-user demand (Ryan, 2002). And as Matkin put it in 2002: "The roof clearly has caved in on several efforts of prominent universities and colleges that entered the online game early with large investments and big plans. The headlines that two or three years ago announced with great fanfare the formation of large-scale and well-financed online learning partnerships have been followed in the past year with equally prominent headlines announcing 'restructuring', 'refocusing', and 'realignment' strategies in these joint ventures" (Matkin, 2002, p. 1). The marketization of online education programs and the immense failures associated with many for-profit ventures in this field in the last decade are discussed further on in Chapter 5.

An additional factor in miscalculating the costs of utilizing the new technologies relates to the underestimation of the high expenses of setting up an appropriate infrastructure for e-learning, its ongoing maintenance, and its wastage management. Setting up an appropriate infrastructure for the effective utilization of the digital technologies in any university or college requires large investments. The computer hardware is still quite expensive, and its rapid change and the need for its frequent replacement increase the expenses entailed. The initial costs of the basic infrastructure needed for operating e-learning is by no means a trivial issue. Lower development/delivery costs have also been challenged by the high cost of software development and, in many instances, demand for face-to-face tutorial support for remote online activities. It has become clear in the last decade that online learning induces ongoing and significant infrastructure costs (OECD, 2005). This implies that many conditions that could lead to a higher cost-efficiency of e-learning compared to conventional learning are not met. Mackintosh (2006) argues that both research and e-learning are costly activities. The adoption of e-learning on campuses places increased pressure on the university budget and therefore it has a direct impact on the sustainable economics of the institution, and on both its teaching and research agenda.

Not only the infrastructure, but also the maintenance of e-learning is costly. It is of tremendous importance to establish support systems for both students and teachers who use the digital technologies. As discussed in Chapter 2, the induction of the teaching faculty into the new technologies necessitates ongoing professional and technical support and the establishment of special centers for course development (Bates, 1999, 2001, 2005; Brindley et al., 2004; Guri-Rosenblit, 2004). Ongoing support is also needed for students, particularly weak students (Brindley et al., 2004; Collis and Moonen, 2001; Guri-Rosenblit, 1999a, 2005a; Littleton and Light, 1999; Scott et al., 2002; Somekh and Davis, 1997; Tait and Mills, 2003).

In addition to the high expenses associated with setting up an appropriate infrastructure for e-learning and keeping up its maintenance, the wastage of the outdated hardware turns to be an unexpected additional cost. Getting rid of outdated computers poses financial, environmental and ethical challenges (Carlson, 2003a). In 2003, the University of Minnesota, for instance, spent more than $100,000 for the demanufacturing of old computers - to pull out valuable steel, aluminium, copper and the chips that contain gold, and to get rid in an appropriate way from the many poisons that computers contain. During the boom of technology in education, colleges bought computers by the truckload. Now the institutions have to be careful how they throw those aging computers away. In some USA states, such as California, New Jersey, Massachusetts, Oregon, Virginia and South Carolina, legislators have proposed or passed laws that ban the disposal of electronic waste and outline how to treat large quantities of hazardous materials which include computer monitors, televisions and other electronics. Electronic waste is regarded now as the next big environmental issue. Old computers compose 10% of solid-waste stream in the USA, but computer related waste is growing as three times as fast as any other kind. The number of computers retired in 2002 was 40 million, and the number of obsolete computers was believed to be nearly 300 million in 2004 (ibid). Many universities and colleges have not decided yet how to deal with their electronic waste and how to sponsor this activity. In sum, it is definitely not very easy to turn e-learning into a profit making activity. Although the promise of online distance education has been great, cost constraints continue to limit the parameters of its delivery (Arafeh, 2004).

Many agree that much work needs to be done related to the costs of the digital technologies' implementation in education environments (Arafeh, 2004; Hulsmann, 2004; Perraton, 2000; Trucano, 2005). The lack of reliable costs data in virtually all areas is quite striking. Few good, rigorous cost studies on the applications of technologies in higher education settings exist in developing countries, and surprisingly also very few such studies have been conducted in OECD countries as well (Perraton, 2000). Arafeh (2004) stressed an important issue related to investigating the costs of e-learning. Most cost studies neglect to ask perhaps the most fundamental question: 'Can you reach the same educational goals and objectives in a different manner at less cost without using ICTs?' Evidently, before large scale investments in online education are performed, much more work has to be done on the costs issue.

In face of the high costs associated currently with some applications of the digital technologies, there are some emerging policy recommendations as to how it is possible to cut the relevant costs of e-learning. For instance, the researchers of the OECD study (OECD, 2005) suggest that e-learning could become a less expensive model compared to conventional face-to-face or distance education from a number of different sources, such as: substituting some online provision for on-campus teaching (rather than duplicating it), facilitating increased peer/automated learning, using standard/pre-existing software, drawing on the open standards and learning objects model to increase material re-use and sharing, avoiding duplication of effort, and planning greater course standardization. In any case, re-organization of the digital technologies usage should involve a decrease in course development costs, a decrease in the student/staff ratio or savings due to less facility use (e.g. classrooms).

Chapter 4

DIVERSE HIGHER EDUCATION ENVIRONMENTS

It is misleading to examine the impact of the digital technologies on higher education in generic terms, since the technologies affect differently diverse educational environments. Many studies illustrate the immense diversity between higher education systems and different-type higher education institutions in using various applications of the new technologies. The scale of provision and the strategies of implementation are influenced by various variables: available infrastructure needed for the utilization of the technologies, the economic wealth of the countries, governmental policies, academic cultures, institutional goals, the substantive structure of various disciplines and domains of study, etc. The differential impacts of the information and communication technologies are examined in this chapter in the light of meaningful differences that exist between: developing and developed countries, various national academic cultures and policies, academic versus business cultures, different-type higher education institutions, and diverse subject matters.

DEVELOPING AND DEVELOPED COUNTRIES

There are significant differences in the effect that the advanced technologies are having in different countries, related in large to their economic wealth. Advanced economies have advanced systems of higher education and the appropriate infrastructure needed for the technologies' implementation. In all OECD countries, state/national governments play a significant role in the strategic direction and funding of higher education in general, and e-learning in particular (OECD, 2005; UNESCO, 2003, 2005). The digital technologies are of great importance to tertiary education in developing countries: they have the potential to expand access and improve the quality of instruction and learning at all levels, they might vastly broaden access to information and data resources, and greatly assist in professional training (Hawkins, 2002; Perraton, 2000; South African Institute of Distance Education, 2004). However, the fact is that the advanced technologies are not yet fully operational in many areas, and friendly Internet access is not widely available in most developing countries. The setting of infrastructure is particularly crucial for developing countries. According to a study of the World Bank in 1999, developing countries comprised 80.4% of the world population, but only 5.95% of Internet hosts. Only 12% of the world population was living in 1999 in US and Canada, but these two countries hosted 65.3% of the Internet hosts. Sub-Saharan African countries together had only one Internet user per 5,000 people as compared to Europe and North America where the proportion was one user for every six inhabitants (World Bank, 2002a, pp. 15-16).

Obviously, there is still a long way to go for setting appropriate infrastructures in the developing world for the effective utilization of the communication and information technologies. Bates, who was asked by the International Institute for Educational Planning of UNESCO to recommend national strategies for implementing e-learning in post-secondary education in various parts of the world, stressed in his report on National Strategies for E-learning in Post-Secondary Education and Training that: "E-learning is heavily dependent on appropriate technological infrastructure already being in place for commerce or government reasons. Stable electricity and reliable and moderately priced Internet access is a necessary condition for e-learning" (Bates, 2001, p.113). Until there is a basic and reliable infrastructure in place, e-learning is unlikely to be a realistic or practical choice for learners in those countries that lack the appropriate infrastructure (Bates, 2007; World Bank, 2002a).

Paradoxically, most higher education institutions in OECD countries do not consider the digital technologies as central to the teaching and learning process, as discussed earlier in Chapter 2, whereas many education initiatives in developing countries seek, at least in their rhetoric, to place the information and communication technologies as central to teaching and learning (Trucano, 2005). Broadcast technologies such as radio and television have a much greater penetration than the Internet throughout much of the developing world, and the substantial gap is not expected to be closed soon (Bates, 2001, 2005, 2007; Mena, 2007; OECD, 2005; Trucano, 2005; World Bank, 2000, 2002a,b). However, many policy makers and academics in developing countries view the broadcasting technologies as less attractive, and their usage is seen as mainly reinforcing of traditional learning models, unlike the digital technologies with their advanced and sophisticated capacities. But in reality the 'older' media are often more suitable for many of the developing countries, and they also provide greater economies-of-scale as compared to the digital technologies. Bates concluded that: "Those countries that are not yet ready for the knowledge-based economy are probably not yet ready for e-learning" (Bates, 2001, p. 111), and he suggested that those countries with large numbers of students unable to access the final years of secondary or higher education should adopt the industrial model of the distance teaching universities, that provides the best route for mass education, rather than design e-learning frameworks. For many developing countries, the industrial model of distance education still provides a much cheaper and more feasible possibility than trying to adopt the new digital technologies.

China, India and Some other Emerging Economies

It is important to keep in mind however that there is a huge variety among developing countries. A study by the International Labour Office found that the new technologies had a most positive impact in some developing countries. Brazil, China, Costa Rica, India, Malaysia, and Romania have successfully created - with the help of relatively effective education systems - information technology niches to allow them to compete in the global market (World Bank, 2002a). Some of the developing countries constitute economies on the rise which are rapidly expanding their higher-education systems, with China probably witnessing the biggest expansion of student numbers in history (Caelis International, 2004; Economist, 2005a). In the 1980s, only 2%-3% of school-leavers in China went to university. In 2003, the figure was

17%. The watershed year was 1999, when the number of students enrolled in Chinese universities jumped by almost half.

China now represents a huge market for international operation, even as its national government attempts to build its own system of higher education (Douglass, 2005: Economist, 2005a; Farrell and Wachholz, 2003). Currently, there are not enough existing higher education institutions in China to absorb the growing demand for higher education. China welcomes outside providers in its push to increase the size and scope of higher education access, at least for the time being. Chinese are forging many collaborative ventures with western universities. The Chinese are using joint ventures with foreign universities in much the same way as Chinese companies use joint ventures with foreign companies. In opening its higher education market, the Chinese government makes certain demands. Foreign universities must partner with a Chinese university: half of the members of governing boards for the venture must be from China, and the venture cannot seek a profit as an objective (Garrett, 2004a). Digital technologies are employed in many of these joint ventures.

India as well portrays an impressive expansion of its higher education system, particularly the booming of a private sector. Some of the private ventures were just low level diploma mills. In February 2005, India's Supreme Court ordered the closure of nearly 100 private universities because of quality concerns (Tilak, 2008). Still, the best private universities are doing admirable work, responding to unmet demand for technical and managerial education, encouraging entrepreneurs to pour millions into a sector that has traditionally been starved of funds. An example of a successful private university in India is Rai University, established by Vinay Rai, a telecoms and steel magnate and an entrepreneur in higher education. Rai University bills itself as 'India's best private university', with 16 campuses across the country connected by a rich technological infrastructure (Economist, 2005a). Not only private universities, but also a growing brand of successful private companies is engaged in India in training high tech personnel for India and for export abroad. NIIT, a computer-training company, has 40 wholly owned centers and more than 1,000 franchised operations, and is expanding to America and Britain. It has established a research-and-development department to discover the most effective teaching methods. It has also created links with Citibank to enable students to take out loans to pay fees. The company has become such a brand name that some advertisements in the matrimonial pages of the Times of India specify graduates of NIIT.

In addition to the emerging economies of China and India there are other countries that try to enhance their knowledge economy through collaboration with leading research universities, particularly from the US and the UK, and by reinforcing their technological infrastructure. Singapore is determined to turn itself into a 'knowledge island' by establishing close relations with 15 partners, including such elite institutions from the US as Stanford, Cornell and Duke Medical School. Extensions of leading universities have been established also in rich Gulf countries, such as Dubai and Qatar. Dubai has established a 'knowledge village' with 13 foreign universities, and Qatar has established an 'educational city' with four extensions, largely for the benefit of Middle Easterners who want a western education but think they may no longer be welcome in America (Economist, 2005a). The digital technologies play an important role in all of these extensions.

Digital Divide

Most of the developing countries are nowadays still backward, and do not possess the appropriate infrastructure for utilizing the wide spectrum of the digital technologies' capabilities, nor do they possess the funds to invite extensions of leading universities to operate on their grounds. Many scholars relate to the danger of the digital divide which the increasing reliance on the digital information and advanced communication technologies has introduced. In the mid 1990s the term 'digital divide' surfaced as a means for politicians and social scientists to describe the socio-economic chasm between individuals, societies and nations who have access to computers and those who do not (Heppel, 1989; Warschauer, 2003). Great strides have been made in the last decade by government agencies, educational institutions, individual communities, and non-profit organizations to bridge the digital divide (Bridges Organization, 2003; Cooper and Weaver, 2003; De Ferranti and Perry, 2003; Dupin-Bryant, 2006; Fink and Keneny, 2003; Hargittai, 2002; Kidd and Chen, 2008; Lenhart, 2003; Mack, 2001; Norris, 2001).

The 'digital divide' has several dimensions. Within a given region, some countries have a stronger technological infrastructure than others. Within countries, technological change often means that groups which were already disadvantaged or excluded, such as - low-income families, rural populations, women, minorities, and the elderly – fall rather behind. In the UK, for instance, only 4% of households in the poorest income quintile were connected to the Internet in 1999, compared with 43% in the top quintile, and the gap is increasing every year (World Bank, 2002a). In the US the proportion of Afro-American families that were connected to the Internet in 1999/2000 was half as compared to white families (OECD, 2001, p. 149).

Particularly, among the developing countries, the digital divide sets apart the technologically more advanced countries from the less advanced ones. Whereas a few African countries with small populations still lack even one Internet host, in Singapore 98% of households use the Internet. The technological divide is reflected in the number of personal computes per 1,000 inhabitants. Less than 1 in Burkina Faso, compared with 27 in South Africa, 38 in Chile, and 348 in Switzerland. In Sub-Saharan Africa the number of Internet hosts per 1,000 population ranges from 0.01% in Burkina Faso to 3.82 in South Africa (World Bank, 2002, pp. 14-15). Gladieux and Swail, in examining the problems associated with the operation of the African Virtual University, emphasized that explicit attention needs to be given to equity considerations so that the new technologies which "shatter geographical barriers may do so without erecting new ones and worsening the digital divide" (Gladieux and Swail, 1999, p. 17).

Africa

Schachter et al. overviewed distance teaching in Africa, with a focus on the digital technologies, in order to examine how distance education may provide some directions to the challenges facing the resource-starved and ill-supported higher education in Sub-Sharan Africa where the loss of professionals through out-immigration (brain drain) is a serious and depressing problem. They concluded that: "For most institutions in Africa the cost of setting up the necessary infrastructure remains prohibitive" (Schachter et al., 2006, p. 171). The challenge of setting up an appropriate infrastructure for utilizing the new technologies is further exacerbated by the dearth of appropriately skilled technical support staff.

Several international and Non-Governmental Organizations, such as the Commonwealth of Learning, UNESCO, the World Bank, as well as a number of European governments, have been prominent in facilitating and funding various endeavors purporting to advance the use of advanced technologies in African higher education. The World Bank constitutes nowadays an important vehicle for assisting many poor developing countries to rebuild and strengthen their higher education systems. Not so long ago the World Bank was reluctant to spend on higher education, and viewed such a spending as both economically inefficient and socially regressive. Now many development economists are warming to higher education, pointing to the demand for graduates and to the positive effect of university education on the economy of developing countries (Economist 2005a; UNESCO, 2002, 2003, 2005; World Bank, 2000, 2002a, b).

The World Bank has founded in 1997 the African Virtual University as a pilot project. Its goal was to establish partnerships with key African universities and to offer credit courses and non-credit seminars in the Sub-Saharan Africa, primarily utilizing video-conferencing technology. On completion of the pilot phase, the African Virtual University converted into an independent NGO offering accredited programs using a modular, digital library to provide more access to scholarly publications and share African research results, connectivity assistance for its partner institutions and a distance learning portal to all African universities. Since most libraries in African countries are generally resource starved or very dated and with deteriorating infrastructures, on-line digital libraries, such as those of the African Virtual University, provide a much needed solution, once widespread and reliable connectivity is achieved. But to achieve the connectivity is no small problem. Computers can be utilized efficiently if they are easily accessible by potential learners. The initial assumption that a handful of computers put in several study centers can serve thousands of students that will line up to use them for a short while has not been substantiated in reality.

The International Institute for Capacity Building in Africa (IICBA) provides another example of an interesting project that was established in 1999 by UNESCO. The goal of IICBA has been to develop the capacities of African institutions in the fields of teacher education, curriculum development, educational policy, planning and management, and distance education (Schachter et al., 2006). IICBA applies the digital technologies in the provision of services and has developed several electronic library resources. It is expected that by 2015 all universities and colleges in Africa will be connected to the Internet.

Some scholars argue that no matter how the technical infrastructure will be upgraded throughout Africa in the next decade, it will have little effect, or even a negative effect of increasing the digital divide within the nations, unless a concurrent development takes place in human resources (Schachter et al., 2006; Wagner et al., 2004; World Bank, 2000, 2002b). The Early Childhood Development Virtual University constitutes an attempt of developing human leadership in the field of early childhood development in African countries. It is a three-year Masters degree in early childhood development, which began in 1999. This blended program operating out of the University of Victoria in Canada and developed with direct funding of the World Bank, has its antecedents in an aboriginal Early Childhood Development program that Dr Alan Pence and colleagues developed in the late 1980s, as well as UNICEF supported face-to-face seminars and a World Bank supported conference held subsequently in Africa. From its initial development proposal through a summative evaluation conducted by the World Bank in 2005, the focus of the program has been on achieving broad and far-reaching impacts through the vehicle of intensive work with a multi-country cohort of leaders, and potential leaders, identified by their own countries (Schachter et al., 2006).

Schachter et al. conclude that looking to the future of e-learning for the next decade or more in African and other Majority World countries: "We can posit that there will be increased connectivity which will, in turn, contribute to the growth and sustainability of locally-based and international networks of scholars and practitioners. Increasingly, learners from developing countries will benefit from a growing resource base, e.g., the expansion of open source repositories for curriculum and other learning materials as well as freely accessible digital libraries" (Schachter et al., 2006, p.181).

The Potential of the Mobile Technologies in Developing Countries

A major challenge nowadays in the implementation process of the digital technologies mainly in developed countries is to achieve the appropriate integration of the digital technologies into the education systems and institutions at large, and to ensure that the new technologies become agents of expanded access and equity and increase educational opportunities for all, not just for the wealthy and the technologically privileged (Clancy et al., 2007).

The emerging mobile technologies are thought to hold much promise for providing connectivity to remote areas, particularly in developing countries. Motlik (2008) argues that reliance on e-learning methods does not appear to work well in most developing countries so far, and that the Internet applications seem to be a poor fit for most of the Asian and African countries. Even in the emerging and successful economies of Korea and China, recent reports show that the adoption of Internet-based learning has been fraught with problems: Lack of necessary technology, lack of Internet accessibility, lack of online resources, high costs, and lack of credibility for online degrees (Baggaley and Belawati, 2007). Motlik claims that it will be a mistake to continue investing in Internet-based education in Asia and in Africa. Just as North America has been a driving force behind Internet-based distance education, Asia will play the leading role in mobile-learning (m-learning). Motlik believes that the mobile learning methods, mainly the use of cell phones, hold great promise for developing countries.

Qiu and Thompson go so far to claim that the mobile technologies form a new-type reality that differs meaningfully from the Internet reality: "Asia offers excellent cases for the exploration of something one may call 'mobile modernities', i.e., a particular set of technological, social and cultural realities that are supplementary and antithetical to the singularly conceptualized 'Internet modernity'" (Qiu and Thomson, 2007, p. 898). Qiu and Thompson believe that Asia will be the driving force in educational uses of the mobile phones owing to its willingness to band together under a unified digital network, unlike the situation in North America which lacks a unified digital network and still relies mainly on an analogue system.

Visser and West (2005) believe that there is also a great promise for the use of mobile phones in education in Africa. The mobile phone diffusion is not nearly as high in Africa as in Asia, but it is on the rise. However, projects utilizing the mobile technologies today are for the most part in pilot or planning stages, and face many regulatory hurdles (Attewell, 2005; Hamilton, 2003; Trucano, 2005; Visser and West, 2005; World Bank, 2000, 2002a,b). Hopefully, some of the existent obstacles might be overcome in the future.

National Academic Cultures and Policies

Different academic cultures in various national settings and diverse government policies do affect to great extent the nature and scope of the technologies' integration in different countries, as is the case in the implementation of any other innovation or reform in higher education. Clearly, each national higher education system has its own peculiar features and qualities (Guri-Rosenblit, 2006; Postman, 1993; Taylor and Harris, 2005). As Burton Clark put it: "National systems of higher education vary in their organization and structure...Different national structures then produce different responses to common trends and demands. The structure of a national system is generally the primary determinant of the direction and intensity of change within it, and the degree of success in deliberate reforms" (Clark, 1986, p. 259).

The complexity of cultural and political differences between nations is of tremendous importance in explaining and predicting the success or failure of implementing innovations, such as the digital technologies. A successful university in one country can turn to be a total failure in a different cultural context (Clancy et al., 2007; Guri-Rosenblit, 2006). For instance, Phoenix University, the largest for-profit distance teaching university in the US, pulled out in 2005 of the UK market because of a lack of enrollment demand. Its ethos of operation and the structure of its courses have not been attractive in the British context. And vice versa, the UK Open University, a most successful distance teaching university in Britain, attempted to form alliances in the US market, only to find that its style of teaching and curriculum structure do not appeal to the American market. It pulled out this venture in 2003 (Douglass, 2005; Garret, 2004b).

Mass Media in Distance Teaching Universities

When the large distance teaching universities were established in the early 1970s, they have adopted different policies in relation to open access and the utilization of available technologies, taking into consideration the prevalent academic culture of each national higher education system in which they operated. The UK Open University, the Israeli Open University, and Athabasca University in Canada adopted an open admission policy, whereas

FernUniversität in Germany and UNED in Spain decided to require the same entry requirements as the conventional universities. They did so, because they feared that they will be looked down by their counterparts, if they practiced an open access policy (Guri-Rosenblit, 1999a).

The large scale distance teaching universities also related differently to the utilization of mass communication technologies. Television in the 1970s was the queen of the media, and the new distance teaching universities were expected to harness the technology of mass communication to the purpose of widening access to higher education. The initial purpose of establishing the UK Open University was based on the idea of mobilizing the BBC for the transmission of lectures throughout Britain. Indeed, the UK Open University went into official partnership with the BBC for nearly thirty years, though its main medium of instruction has been based to this date on self-study printed materials.

Interestingly, though Germany was a leader in mass communication technologies in the 1970s, the FernUniversität decided from the outset not to broadcast on television or radio, but rather to stay mainly with print technology, in order to be as similar as possible to other German universities. Bartels and Peters reveal the underlying justification behind the decision of the FernUniversität to concentrate mainly on the print medium: "The deliberate choice of printed materials as a central medium is explained by the fact that a selection of media and the best media mix is not only a matter of technological development of media of know-how, but also a social acceptance, professional traditions and financial feasibility" (Bartels and Peters, 1986, pp. 109-110). Peters, the founding president of the FernUniversität, decided that it is best for the future of his new university to stay as conservative as possible and adopt the principle of 'wait and see' attitude towards the mass media technologies. This policy was adopted deliberately in order to be acknowledged as a respectable new university adhering to the existing cultural norms in the German higher education, and not endangering its reputation through collaboration with television broadcasts, that were associated in those days mainly with entertainment (Guri-Rosenblit, 1999a).

Government Policies

Government policies in relation to the digital technologies play a prominent role in shaping the attitudes of higher education institutions in any given national jurisdiction towards online learning, alliances with the business and corporate world, and transnational education. Marked differences can be observed nowadays between government policies in English speaking countries and other nationalities in harnessing the digital technologies to promote transnational education, and expand the higher education boundaries beyond the national jurisdictions.

In the globalized world we live in, it is quite obvious that English has become the *lingua franca* of the academic world, and this trend will intensify in the future. It is not merely the major language of conferences, academic publications and research journals, but it also has become an important vehicle for promoting and widening transnational education, which means that in the near future millions of students will either study outside their national jurisdictions, or study towards degrees offered by external extensions, or through distance education. It is not by accident that the English speaking countries are the main advocates of transnational education and push towards the finalization of the GATS (General Agreement on Trade in Services). In the GATS framework education is being categorized as a service commodity subject to international trade rules. The US, the UK and Australia are currently the world's strongest providers of transnational education. Education and training services rank among the US top five in-services exports, and among the top ten of general exports in Australia. The involvement of the US Department of Commerce, the US International Trade Committee, the National Committee for International Trade in Education (US), the Industry Commission (Australia), and the Department for Trade and Industry in the UK clearly demonstrate that the policy statements from these countries employ an explicit vocabulary in relation to trade of higher education as a commodity. Not surprisingly, these countries are the most active contestants of trade restrictions and lead the debate in favour of the attempts to eliminate existing barriers to international trade in education (Economist, 2005a,b,c,d).

A Prime Minister's Initiative launched in 1999 by Tony Blair in the UK encouraged universities to engage in a strategy of international competitiveness through both attracting international students to British universities and exporting higher education programs throughout the world.

The UK Government has funded the British Council (with offices in 110 countries) to launch a major five-year worldwide marketing initiative to encourage international students to study in the UK or to enroll in extensions of UK universities in dozens of countries (Clancy et al., 2007). Also the Australian government has invested in the last decade to increase meaningfully its transnational students. It aims to have one million transnational students in 2025 out of a total of seven million transnational students that are projected to be at that time. Australian universities were sponsored by the government to launch many off-shore activities. Out of 38 higher education institutions in Australia, 27 universities have offshore programs in the burgeoning higher education market in China and in the Pacific Rim (Economist, 2005a,c).

Advantages of Anglo-Saxon Countries

The Anglo-Saxon countries are taking advantage of several cultural and historical attributes, characterizing the structure of their higher education systems, to lead the trend of transnational and globalized higher education. Van der Wende (2001) lists some of the advantages inherent in the academic cultures of the Anglo-Saxon countries: English as the academic *lingua franca*, flexible degree structures, student-centered approaches, strong traditions in distance learning, off-shore delivery strategies (especially in the UK and Australia), differential fee systems which provide incentives to institutions to employ active marketing strategies. An additional important factor is obviously the use of information and communication technologies, which enable the cross-border delivery of programs through university extensions and the establishment of transnational virtual universities (Enders and Fulton, 2002; Guri-Rosenblit, 2006).

Interestingly, since September 11th 2001, and the restrictions on student visas, it seems that America's leadership in the domain of transnational education is under challenge. The Institute of International Education reported that the number of foreign students on American campuses declined by 2.4% in 2003/04, the first time the number has gone down in 30 years. Foreign applications to American graduate schools fell by 28% in 2004, and actual enrollment dropped by 6% (Douglass, 2005). Lestz (2005) offered to organize a new educational entity that will reconnect the American higher education with the world. He suggested to establish a university without walls or buildings or a standing faculty, which might be called 'Profs Without Borders'. It will be a NGO entity born out of the university milieu. Such an organization would pool the talents of some of the most able professors and specialists in American universities to work on projects from which an enormous harvest of good could come for both the US and mainly its role as a leader in transnational higher education. Obviously the digital technologies will provide the necessary infrastructure for connecting the professors and experts, dispersed in different universities.

Continental European Countries

Unlike the Anglo-Saxon countries which have adopted an explicit competitive approach to the internationalization of higher education, most of the continental European countries seem to pursue a different approach, which is more cooperative in nature. According to van der Wende (2001) this may be explained from a political and a value-based perspective. In many European countries, free access to higher education is seen as an established right, which conflicts with the view of higher education as a commodity to be traded on a world market. The rationale to compete internationally may be absent, or even undesirable in many European countries, such as France, Italy and Germany. Where higher education funding is virtually completely funded by the state, no fees can be charged to students, and limited autonomy is granted to institutions, with few incentives and no real options for competing internationally (Economist, 2005e,f). Not surprisingly, most continental European countries pursue a cooperative approach to internationalization, which in terms of international learning and experience is compatible with the traditional and cultural values of European academia.

The Bologna Process, which has started in 1999, aims at harmonizing higher education systems through Europe until 2010. The main means to achieve the harmonization is to enhance the transparency of European higher education, in particular the comparability of higher education degrees and qualifications. This is a most complicated process due to differences in national regulations, levels of autonomy, degree structures and, of course, the use of many languages.

However, one of the major goals of the Bologna Process has been not only to consolidate and harmonize the European higher education systems, but also to enhance the international competitiveness of European higher education, mainly *vis-à-vis* the American higher education. Such a goal promotes competitiveness in the continental European countries. Furthermore, there is already a competitive market in many European countries, enhanced by the proliferation of many private providers, mainly in niche areas, such as business administration, international law, computer science (Levy, 2008). This bottom-up expansion of private higher education in Europe took place because some countries were unable to meet the rising demand for studies in attractive areas of high market demand. Where national higher education systems have not responded to the widening and increasingly diversifying demand for higher education, a market of foreign providers of higher education in Europe has been established. Many of the new private providers offer online courses for part-time and lifelong students (OECD, 2005; UNESCO, 2005).

Unique Attributes of the US Higher Education Culture

Within the Anglo-Saxon countries, it is worth relating to some unique characteristics of the US higher education that set it apart from all other higher education systems worldwide, and have a meaningful impact on shaping the nature of online education in American universities. Three unique cultural attributes of the American higher education are: A proclaimed service mission to the society through extensions; weak federal government intervention in setting higher education policies; and a strong tradition of alliances with the business world.

US universities have created extensions more than 100 years ago, through which they have offered new programs, to help meet public needs without interfering with core academic programs. The Morrill Act of 1862 has created the system of land-grant universities, and the Smith-Lever Act of 1914 established the Cooperative Extension System in the US (Rasmussen, 1989). Each state extension service is headquartered at a land-grant university. The underlying philosophy of the extension system was to "help people help themselves" by "taking the university to the people" (ibid, p. vii). The purpose of the extension system was to establish strong connections between the universities and their surrounding environments to enable to transfer useful and practical information on subjects related to agriculture, home economics and other relevant fields. Land-grant universities and university extensions are uniquely American institutions. No other country has focused such attention on the practical and applied dimension of higher education by applying the knowledge base of the land-grant universities to real life laboratories where people live and work. In the University of California, for example, extension programs date back to the late 1890s and today enroll more than 200,000 students. Not accidentally, extension programs are nowadays the common providers of online courses among many American universities (Douglass, 2001).

The degree of governmental intervention and regulation in university affairs constitutes an important factor in the adoption of changes and innovations in higher education, and in shaping the climate for entrepreneurship and collaboration between the academic and the business worlds. Many claim that the great success of the US higher education system is closely related to the fact that the federal government plays a limited part in higher education institutions, as opposed to many European countries that are tightly monitored by regulatory controls linked to funding (Douglass, 2005; Economist, 2005g; Trow, 1999, 2001).

The US does not have a central plan for its universities. It does not treat its academics as civil servants, as do France and Germany. Instead, universities have a wide range of patrons, from state governments to religious bodies, from fee-paying students to generous philanthropists. The unique interrelations between the academic institutions and the corporate world in the USA are non-existent in any other country. The generous donations and endowments of the business world and private alumni to American universities are of envy in all other countries, and are hard to imitate, because they are built on strong cultural roots that have been cultivated for centuries in the American society (Guri-Rosenblit, 2006; Levy, 2008). Such a culture is most inductive for entrepreneurship (Clark, 1998; Vest, 2007).

The US has pioneered the art of forging links between academia and industry (Rothblatt, 1997, 2007; Trow, 2001; Vest, 2007). It is no wonder then that many of the large technological ventures in the last decade took place in the US. More than 170 universities had in 2003 'business incubators' of some sort, and dozens operated their own venture funds (Douglass, 2005). However, not everything is rosy in the collaborative ventures between the academia and the corporate world, since they operate in quite different cultures. The clashes between these two cultures are discussed below.

ACADEMIC VERSUS BUSINESS CULTURES

Many alliances were created in the last decade between the corporate world and some leading research institutes in the US and in some other countries. Many of these ventures failed to fulfill their initial goals. Deep differences between the organizational cultures of the academic and the business world explain part of the problems in some of the joint ventures. The research interests of the business sector versus the academic world are different. Their expectations, perceptions and professional lingos reflect distinct working milieux. The decision making apparatus in the business world differs meaningfully from that of the universities. Corporations are ready to invest large sums of money both in research and in inviting tailor-made training programs, but they want the end-products to be delivered exactly on time, and decisions made fast (Matkin, 2002). These are not exactly the values and operational procedures that characterize the academic life. Decisions at any given academic department have to be approved by several committees, and large amounts of time are needed for reflection and deliberation (Guri-Rosenblit, 2005b).

In addition, many corporate trainers claimed that they were frequently disappointed from the quality of the programs they got from universities. Some of the generic online courses they have purchased were simply boring and could not engage learners sufficiently to maintain interest (Ryan, 2002). Too often text was shoveled on screen, animated with a few trite graphics, and tested with memory-recall quizzes. But, it is also obvious that more customer-tailored programs increase development costs, and eventually eliminate the savings promised by mass-market distributed learning.

Some other business leaders claimed that the structure of the university courses does not fit their rhythm and needs. The ponderous nature of some for-credit university courses appear to be unattractive to many in the business environment, as NYUOnline found prior to its demise. It reduced its 13-week semester-length courses based on university rhythms, to 6-week modules, in a desperate attempt to cater to short attention spans and fast-finish mentalities of the corporate world. Industry and the business world prefer just-in-time training rather than concerted programs of study (Matkin, 2002; Ryan, 2002). Such disappointment led many large corporations to establish their own universities geared to train their personnel in close coordination with their professional demands.

Furthermore, the research interests of the business sector versus the academic world are different. Corporate sponsors are attaching strings to their donations in order to prevent competitors from free-riding on their research, such as forcing scientists to delay publication or even blank out crucial passages from published papers. When Novartis, a Swiss pharmaceutical giant, agreed to invest $25m in Berkeley's College of Natural Resources, for example, it stipulated that it should get a first look at much of the research carried out by the plant and microbial biology department (Economist, 2005d).

It follows that in collaborative research ventures on the implementation of the electronic technologies between universities and the corporate sector it is of tremendous importance to define the major goals of each party, the anticipated end-products, the status of the intellectual property gained through the research, and the terms of publishing the final results and conclusions. Without paying careful attention to the underlying arguments behind contradictory claims and anticipations, the discourse on the potential use of digital technologies might turn confused and frustrating, and even lead to law suits.

The growing impact of the business culture on the academic world is reflected in the last decades by the emergence of new for-profit providers in higher education that operate as businesslike corporations. The number of corporate universities in the US, which provide education for their parent companies, has grown from 400 in the mid-1980s to more than 2,000 today (Economist, 2005h). Some of these institutions, such as the McDonald's Hamburger University, do not deserve the name 'university', but others, such as those set up by Microsoft and Schwab, are considered as more serious providers of professional education. A growing number of corporate universities are awarding degrees or professional diplomas in conjunction with traditional universities. A collaborative venture between Stanford University and Volkswagen Automotive University, signed in May 2005, provides an example of a collaboration between a prestigious elite university with a leading corporate university. According to this agreement, employees of Volkswagen-Uni, an institution of postgraduate education run by the

Volkswagen corporation, will spend a year working and researching industrial design at Stanford University (Borek, 2005). Two Stanford professors will give lectures and courses at Volkswagen-Uni. Volkswagen's research lab in Palo Alto participates also in this project. Prof. Hans Ulrich Gumbrecht explains why this is a fair trade-off: "Auto-Uni hopes to profit from Stanford's academic expertise and prestige as an institution, which it wants to learn. Stanford, I assume, hopes to develop interesting collaboration in high-tech with Volkswagen, through the university" (ibid).

The University of Phoenix is America's largest for-profit university (and indeed US largest university), with over 280,000 students, 239 campuses and various offshoots around the world, including some in China and India (University of Phoenix, 2008). In the early 1990s it became among the first universities to offer degrees online, and the Internet is now integral to most of its teaching, mainly through the blended mode.

The University of Phoenix is designed to cater for the needs of working adults, who make up 95% of its students. The emphasis is on practical subjects, such as business administration and management, nursing and health care, education, technology, psychology, criminal justice, psychology human services, that might help them with their careers. The business orientation of University of Phoenix is clearly reflected in its logistic organization. The classes are organized mainly at the afternoons to fit in with busy schedules. One of the university's golden rules is that there should be plenty of parking lots for students coming to study at the afternoons in a study center, and that students should be able to get from their cars to their classrooms in five minutes (Economist, 2005h).

The University of Phoenix was the brainchild of John Sperling, a Cambridge-educated economist and professor-turned-entrepreneur, (University of Phoenix, 2008). When he was teaching in San Jose State University in the early 1970s, Mr Sperling noticed that adult students got scant attention from universities designed to teach mainly students aged 18-22. That, he felt, was not only unfair but also unwise: in the new economy, workers might have to keep going back to university to update or improve their skills. He saw a growing need for institutions that were sensitive to learning characteristics and life situations of the working adult population. He designed a different-type university, with several far-reaching innovations, which departed significantly from the prevalent culture of conventional universities, and from the classical status of professors in universities. The first was to concentrate power in the organization. In traditional universities academics enjoy academic freedom to devote as much time as possible to their own research, and in many countries they also are responsible for managing the administrative and economic matters of their universities. In the University of Phoenix the teachers are simply employees. It is the university, not the teachers, that owns the curriculum. Todd Nelson, who was until 2006 the Chairman and CEO of the Apollo Group, responsible for the overall operation of the University of Phoenix, claimed in an interview for *Economist* that such a policy has allowed the university to become a 'learning organization': it is constantly improving its ability to teach by measuring performance and disseminating successful techniques. The only research it cares about is the sort that improves teaching (Economist, 2005h). An additional innovation has been to turn higher education into a for-profit business. The cost of a year's education at Phoenix in 2005, was $9,000, not particularly high for a private university, but the business ethos is unusually pervasive. The Apollo Group spent a staggering $383m on marketing in 2004/5.

The article in the Economist describes one of the University of Phoenix campuses, the Hohokam campus that houses the corporate headquarters of the Apollo Group, the company that owns the university, along with the group's corporate university: "The University of Phoenix's Hohokam campus looks more like a corporate headquarters than a regular university. There is none of the cheerful mess that you associate with student life. The windows are made from black reflecting glass, the corridors are neat and hushed, the grass has been recently cut, there is plenty of parking space for everybody, and security guards in golf carts make sure all the cars are on legitimate business. The university is conveniently close to a couple of motorways, and ten minutes from the airport. But the campus does not just look like a corporate headquarters; it is one" (Economist, 2005h).

Some of the for-profit universities are doing an excellent job in filling market niches, particularly for technical education, but their position in the academic hierarchy remains humble. Strayer University, one of the University of Phoenix's biggest competitors, concentrates on telecommunications and business administration. Concord Law School, owned by Kaplan, which in turn is owned by the *Washington Post*, boasts one of the largest law-school enrollments in the country. All of its teaching is online. Cardean University, the brainchild of Michael Milken, offers online business education, including MBAs (Economist, 2005h). For-profit institutions in the US expect to grow their online learning component faster than any other institutions of higher education, expecting growth rates greater than 40% (Allen and Seaman, 2003).

In the last decade hundreds of new for-profit universities and consortia have been established throughout the world, both in developed and developing countries (Levy, 2008). In Brazil, for instance, in the late 1990s there were fewer than 20 corporate universities. By 2003, however, the number expanded to 150 (Porto and Berge, 2008). Many large private sector corporations such a *Ambev* (beverages), *Accor* (hotels), and *Santander Banespa* (banking) are investing in the development of continuous educational offerings for their staff and executives. In many cases, third party organizations are called upon to offer customized and off-the-shelf corporate training programs. This is the case of the corporate university named *Ibmec* which operates out of Sao Paulo. From 2004 to 2005, *Ibmec* saw demand for its distance education offerings skyrocket by 40%, followed by 30% increase for 2006 (ibid). Porto and Berge claim that most of the corporate universities in Brazil use today Web-based e-learning and virtual environments. These companies' corporate universities "had to bear high initial investment costs in the design and delivery of e-learning, but such investments were subsequently offset with gains in employee productivity and overall performance" (ibid). In some cases, the corporate universities , sensing new market opportunities and growing demand, have created their own 'educational brand' and have moved to offer their services to outside companies and clienteles. The marketization of higher education will be discussed further on in Chapter 5.

DIFFERENT-TYPE INSTITUTIONS

Higher education systems worldwide are vastly diverse and are composed of different type institutions. There are: elite research universities, mass-oriented universities, professional institutes, liberal arts colleges, community colleges, mega distance teaching universities, for-profit training institutions, corporate universities, etc. The academic goals, potential clienteles and organizational infrastructure of each of these institutions are diverse, and these profound differences shape the ways in which the new technologies are mobilized in each context to achieve different end-products (Guri-Rosenblit, 1999b; 2005b, 2006). Curran claims that the most striking characteristic of e-learning strategies adopted by universities is their diversity. E-learning strategies that universities adopt reflect, rather than influence, institutional ethos (Curran, 2004). Various studies illustrate the immense diversity between different-type higher education institutions in using the digital technologies as they are manifested in their program aims, in the extent to which the activities form an integral part of the established academic structures, in the arrangements for management and governance of e-learning activities, and in the pedagogic approach adopted.

A huge diversity of higher education institutions characterizes nowadays both developed and developing countries (Guri-Rosenblit, 2007). A noticeable phenomenon in many developing countries is the proliferation of different kinds of universities. A few years ago most universities in the developing world were much the same: designed for the elite and dominated by the state. Now there is a great variety. The biggest change is the emergence of a for-profit sector that concentrates on subjects such as accounting and computer skills, and often pioneers educational innovation. Many extensions from developed countries that operate in developing countries utilize the digital technologies, and many private universities were established by business leaders (Dogramaci, 2008; Levy, 2008; Tilak, 2008).

A few of the newly founded private universities have succeeded to establish a respectable academic reputation. Such is the case of Rai University in India, mentioned earlier. Part of its reputation relates to its most comprehensive and updated technological infrastructure which stands out clearly when compared with poor technological infrastructures in public universities, even some of the leading research public universities. An article in the *Economist* in 2005 described the profound differences between the infrastructure of Rai University as compared to Jawaharlal Nehru University, one of India's most distinguished public universities. The contrast is quite striking: "Rai University is spick and span whereas Jawaharlal Nehru University is sprawling and untidy. Rai is full of computers, whereas Jawaharlal Nehru University is resolutely low-tech. Rai's students are determined to take part in the global economy, whereas Jawaharlal Nehru University is plastered with signs protesting against the evils of capitalism" (Economist, 2005a). The example of Rai and Jawaharlal Nehru University demonstrates that immense differences exist between different institutions in many countries, and part of these difference relate to the possession or lack of appropriate technological infrastructures.

An additional sweeping example of immense differences that exist between institutions, in both their needs and attitudes towards the new technologies, is provided by comparing the policies and practices of elite research universities and large scale distance teaching universities. These differences are cross national. Elite research universities are better equipped to utilize many of the information and communication technologies' abilities and qualities as compared to many long-standing distance teaching institutes (Guri-Rosenblit, 2005a,b). But on the other hand, many of the research campus universities feel reluctant to use the new technologies to supplant the face-to-face interaction in a residential university setting, as discussed earlier in the former chapters. The new technologies are applied mainly to enhance the teaching/learning processes in the classroom rather than to substitute the face-to-face interaction.

Why are research universities well-equipped to use the new technologies efficiently, and why do they feel reluctant to use them?

The elite research universities have a favorable ratio of faculty-students and rich financial resources, and therefore they can use the new interactive technologies most effectively for the benefit of their student clienteles and academic faculty. Stanford University, for instance, had in 2001 a ratio of 1:8.2 of faculty to students (Stanford University, 2002) and UCBerkeley of 1:14 (Douglass, 2001), as compared to 1:100 and even more in mass oriented universities (Daniel, 1996; Guri-Rosenblit, 2005b). The new technologies have highlighted the enormous importance of the human interaction in teaching/learning processes. No expert teacher can interact with hundreds, and even dozens, of students. Obviously, many distance teaching universities that employ a very small faculty cannot afford creating small virtual classrooms in which the expert professors will communicate with hundreds of students (Bates, 2001, 2005; Guri-Rosenblit, 2004, 2005b; Hulsmann, 2004). The continuous interaction between students and faculty and amongst students is a most attractive idea and is enabled by the new technologies, but at the same time most difficult, if not impossible, to put forward in highly populated universities with a small number of academic faculty.

The elite research universities have richer resources to lean on and are also much more attractive to the corporate world as compared to mass-oriented and distance teaching universities in developed countries, and even more so in developing countries. Corporate and business enterprises are interested to cooperate with universities in order to enhance research on the new information technologies, and to design tailor-made professional and upgrade training programs for their working force (Adelman, 2000; Ryan, 2002; Xebec McGraw and Training Magazine, 2001). When such giant corporations, as Microsoft and Hewlett were willing to explore and examine in depth some of the advanced technological applications, they naturally approached universities such as Stanford, MIT, Harvard and Cambridge, and rarely had they referred to mass-oriented and distance teaching universities, which by their very nature have less prestigious research capabilities and facilities, and lack the reputation of the leading research universities (Guri-Rosenblit, 2005b).

Paradoxically, though the highly established research universities possess ideal conditions to utilize a wide range of the digital technologies' abilities, they use the technologies most moderately, mainly for add-on function, as was discussed earlier in the former chapters. Reaching out to dozens of thousands of students is naturally not part of the research universities' agenda. They are inclined to stay elitist-oriented for the few and the well-to-do students. Their potential applicants will always exceed the number of places available. Some of the leading research universities have reached out to some distinct populations outside their campuses. But they did so mainly in order to either diversify their resources, or as a service to their surrounding communities.

Unlike the well-to-do research universities, distance teaching universities, as well as some mega universities, that teach dozens of thousands of students, can benefit greatly from the digital technologies' potential. They are greatly interested in extending their target populations, through utilizing the far-reaching abilities of the digital technologies, but most of them encounter many obstacles and hurdles in applying the new technologies. The reason is that most of them lack the appropriate infrastructure and human capital to utilize the new technologies efficiently (Bernath and Hülsmann, 2004; Guri-Rosenblit, 2005a). Such a situation creates an interesting paradox. Those higher education institutions that have the appropriate infrastructures and human capital to use the new technologies most efficiently and effectively, are less inclined to do so, whereas those higher education institutions that badly need the new technologies and might greatly benefit from their applications, often lack the appropriate infrastructure and human capital to harness the power of the new technologies to the benefit of their students, faculty and institutional goals.

Why is it difficult to implement e-learning in large distance teaching institutions?

Quite clearly, the new technologies are most attractive for distance teaching. They have the potential to overcome three major problems of 'traditional' distance education: to rescue the isolated students from their loneliness by providing interaction with teachers, professors and tutors, as well as with other peer students throughout the study process; to provide easy access to libraries and other information resources, which was nearly impossible in the past; and to update the self study materials on an ongoing basis. But, the very basic infrastructure of most large distance teaching universities hinders the wide scale implementation of the digital technologies, as explained below.

Communication: Merits and Problems

The lack of direct teacher-student and student-student communication has been the Achilles heel of distance education for centuries. The new interactive technologies enable universities to overcome this shortcoming. But intensive communication is, by its very nature, labour intensive. The University of Maryland University College University (UMUC, which is the leading public distance teaching university in the US) and the University of Phoenix, presented earlier, are two of the most successful US universities that provide e-learning. Their online classes are restricted from twelve to twenty students to guarantee high levels of interactivity (Ryan, 2002; Trow, 1999; Twigg 2001). The University of Phoenix charges more for its online programs than for tutorials in study centers, since its operators found that the interactivity which students value is not scalable at marginal costs. It turns out that students who study online are willing to pay the additional costs for increased interactivity, but, to this date, the majority of the University of Phoenix students prefer to meet in face-to-face tutorials or choose the blended mode which combines face-to-face and online instruction.

Thus, in theory, enhanced communication in distance education is enabled by the information and communication technologies, but its actualization is much more complicated to achieve. In most large scale distance teaching universities there is a small numbers of faculty members that evidently are unable to communicate with thousands or even with hundreds of students.

Moreover, direct interaction between students and the faculty members who developed the self-study courses necessitates the involvement of the latter in the actual learning/teaching process. But in many distance teaching universities, the faculty members who developed the course, are not involved in its actual teaching (Guri-Rosenblit, 1999a). In other words, the adoption of the interactive technologies requires the abolishment of the very basic characteristic of the industrial model of distance education. Most, if not all, large distance teaching universities, cannot afford to hire many more academics in order to facilitate student-professor interaction in most of their large courses, often taken by thousands of students. Interaction among students and between students and tutors and lower ranks of academic staff has been enhanced in most distance teaching universities, but the synchronous communication between the senior faculty who are responsible for the overall structure and content of any self study course and the students is either extremely limited or non-existent (Guri-Rosenblit, 2005b).

It is no surprise therefore that distance education in most higher education systems is still conducted through the 'old' technologies: mainly print, but also through radio, TV and satellite broadcasts, as discussed already in Chapter 1. The US constitutes an exception. Most of the distance education programs in the US are delivered through e-learning (Allen and Seaman, 2003, 2004; Arafeh, 2004; Bradburn 2002; Gladieux and Swail 1999; US Department of Education 2002). But the US is not exceptional in the pattern of the technologies' applications in campus based universities. As in other parts of the world, most of e-learning in American higher education is not used for distance teaching purposes, but rather for add-on functions to face-to-face encounters.

Access: On Equality and Duplication

Access to libraries and other information resources through the Internet has been used in the last decade at an accelerated pace by members of both distance and campus universities (Kirk and Bartelstein, 1999). More and more libraries are becoming digitalized and going online. But also in this domain of information access, the mega distance teaching universities encounter more difficulties as compared to campus universities. Many of their students, particularly in developing countries, do not have ready access to computers

(Bates, 2001, 2005; Guri-Rosenblit, 2001b, 2005b; World Bank, 2000, 2002a,b).

The egalitarian philosophy of most distance teaching universities, that requires them to provide equality of opportunity to all of their students, also forces them to continue developing their printed self-contained study packages that can be delivered to each student by mail. In other words, catering to large numbers of students, many of whom lack the ability or opportunity to reach Internet facilities and information resources, hinders the distance teaching universities from substituting some of their courses, or parts of any given course, with online materials, and with a built-in reference mechanism in the pre-prepared textbooks. This accounts for the duplication phenomenon. Many distance education institutes develop currently both printed and online versions of courses, and enable their students to choose their preferred mode of study. Such a policy adds on substantial additional costs to the already very expensive process of developing self study materials.

Update of Study Materials: Potential and Difficulties

One of the major problems associated with the development of expensive high quality materials for distance education is the difficulty in updating them. It is tremendously difficult to amend, change and revise materials produced over several years and used in a standardized manner over many years (Daniel, 1996; Guri-Rosenblit, 1999a). Unquestionably, the new technologies and the availability of desktop publishing provide a partial remedy by substantially reducing the time of course production and making the updating of materials less fraught. But in order to be able to update the materials on an ongoing basis, the course developers have to be part of the actual learning/teaching process. Here again the digital technologies challenge the organizational infrastructure of the distance teaching universities and demand a major overhaul of their whole operation (Bates, 1999, 2001, 2005; Guri-Rosenblit, 2001b, 2005b; Peters, 2001).

In campus universities the individual lecturer or tutor in any classroom may alter and redefine reading lists, and set assignments and study tasks in light of the teaching dynamics. However, teaching faculty at most distance teaching universities do not have any latitude whatsoever to make such alterations. The principles of sameness and uniformity apply to assignments and exams as they do to content. In order to employ flexible updating mechanisms, the distance teaching universities have to redefine and restructure their overall teaching mechanisms. The teaching responsibility in most distance teaching universities is distributed among many actors, and exempts most of the senior academic faculty from involvement in the actual study phase. As difficult as the updating task seems to be, the distance teaching universities will have to undertake it, incurring also the additional associated costs of such a process.

In sum, it seems that in spite of the apparent advantages and merits of the digital technologies for distance education, many of the distance teaching institutions lack the appropriate infrastructure and necessary conditions, as well as the human capital, to utilize the full potential of the new technologies. To integrate the electronic media more fully and efficiently into their learning/teaching processes a whole restructuring of their operation is required, and such a process will take time and will necessitate totally new agreements between the large scale distance teaching universities and the national governments that sponsor them.

Diverse Subject-Matters

Obviously, the communication opportunities through e-mail and chat groups, as well as the information retrieval possibilities, can be used across all fields of study. Nevertheless, it is already clear that it is impossible to refer to the overall abilities and characteristics of the digital technologies as to neutral qualities applicable in any subject-matter and for any purpose. The intensity of online learning varies significantly across disciplines. It is already possible to trace some visible trends.

Most of the digital technologies' applications in higher education thus far have taken place in postgraduate courses of business administration, informatics and computer science, engineering, introductory mathematics, statistics, language instruction. As Trow has put it: "They (the technologies) are used primarily to practice skills and transfer defined bodies of knowledge rather than to follow the logic of an argument, appreciate aesthetics, make moral judgments or inquire into ethical dilemmas" (Trow, 1999, p. 202). Particularly, information technology and business/management studies have emerged as the most commonly cited disciplines that make significant use of some form of online education in higher education institutions throughout the globe (Aadelsburger et al., 2002; OECD, 2005; Ponzurick et al., 2000; Wyckoff and Schaper, 2005).

Trucano in his wide scope survey concluded that faculty-led initiatives of technological applications are more common at the postgraduate level and in subjects with a strong disciplinal or sectoral orientation in fields like - engineering, law, medicine, specific areas of business or economics (Trucano, 2005). The leading reasons for faculty-led initiatives in graduate and postgraduate fields, in the above mentioned areas, are mainly a desire to secure additional funding for teaching posts through links with the corporate world, and the concomitant opportunity to secure external funding for related research, including sponsorship of doctoral-research students.

One of the reasons that most of the success stories in online education take mainly place in graduate and postgraduate studies is due to the fact that online education is more compatible for graduate students, who have more experience in the discipline and at the same time need to balance work, home, and study. As pointed out in Chapter 3, students with less experience in a discipline and less background in taking responsibility for aspects of their own learning find it more difficult to study online, and prefer to enroll in a residential university or college.

Pfeffer argued that the new technologies not only assist in teaching existent disciplines, but also create new disciplines of study: "The digital technologies not only change the form of scientific production, they gain increasing influence in research agendas and in the development of academic disciplines. The technologies themselves have become a prominent research topic which even leads to the development of new disciplines and to the foundation of new economic units" (Pfeffer, 2003, p. 4). In all professional domains, the working force need continuous updating of their knowledge and skills, including skill for technology enhanced learning. Lytras et al., in a recent book argue that the new technologies enhance learning based on collaborative working, creativity, multidisciplinarity, adaptiveness, intercultural communication and problem solving that affect all domains in life, including the ways in which traditional subjects have been taught (Lytras et al., 2008)

Almost in any given discipline one can find today books and articles demonstrating how it is advisable to integrate the new technologies both in the research agenda and teaching practices of the discussed field (Carr, 2000;

Donnelly and McSweeney, 2008; Dupin-Brynt, 2006; Heafner, 2004; Herrington and Oliver, 2000; Jones and Issrof, 2005; National Research Council, 2005; Petrides, 2000; Scott et al., 2002). Some publications stress the special importance of relearning, a necessity to update professionals of both new technological tools, and new research methods in their expert fields. An example of such trend provides a recent book edited by Politis (2008) on e-learning methodologies and computer applications in archaeology. The major claim in this book is that data comparison and analysis are critical in the field of archaeology, and the integration of technological advancements such as geographic information systems, intelligent systems and virtual reality reconstruction with the teaching of archaeology is crucial to the effective utilization of resources in this field. Computer applications in archaeology provide tools that enable to transform observations to virtual reality reconstructions in a photorealistic manner. The modeling of the past enables to perform a cognitive walk in new dimensions.

However, the research on the applicability and suitability of the new technologies for the instruction of different type themes is not ripe yet to reach decisive conclusions. Media differ in the extent to which they can represent different kinds of content, since they encompass a wide range of symbol systems, such as verbal printed text, charts and diagrams, sound, moving objects, still pictures, etc. Differences between media in the way in which they combine different symbol systems influence the way in which different media represent content. There is a significant difference between a written text, a televised recording or a simulation of the same experiment in physics, for instance. Many scholars agree that integration of content derived from a variety of sources leads to a deeper understanding of a concept or an idea (Bates, 2005).

Subject matter varies enormously in the way in which information needs to be structured. Knowledge in natural sciences, for instance, is structured differently than knowledge in history, determined by the internal logic and the substantive structure of the subject matter. Postman (1993, in Bates, 2005) argues that there is a strong link between technology and the modes of thinking. Scientific thinking is heavily dependent on the 'objectivity' and linearity of printed material, allowing for descriptions of phenomena, analysis of argument and logic, and communication between scientist through printed journals. If we start to move from linear to lateral thinking we may make some gains in creativity but we may lose some certainty and predictability. Thus there may be strong advantages in combining print with Web-based learning (Bates, 2005, p. 215).

Bates stated that: "If media then vary both in the way they represent information symbolically and in the way they handle the structures required within different subject areas, media which best match the required mode of presentation and the dominant structure of the subject matter need to be selected" (Bates, 2005, p. 57). Consequently, different disciplines will require a different blend of media. This means that subject experts should be deeply involved in decisions about the choice and use of media, at least at a tactical level, to ensure that the chosen media appropriately match the presentational and structural requirements of the subject matter. All technologies have their strengths and weaknesses. There is no 'super-technology'. They therefore need to be combined. To achieve good design usually means working with instructional designers. Each medium and technology has a different range of production skills necessary to exploit its unique features.

Bates (2005) provided an interesting toolkit for guiding the choice of the most efficient and appropriate mix of media for the teaching of various subjects in different contexts. Bates first developed the ACTIONS framework (standing for: Access, Costs, Teaching and Learning, Interactivity and friendliness, Organizational Issues, Novelty and Speed) in 1988 for distance and open learning. More recently, the ACTIONS framework has been amended for choosing technologies for campus-based learning becoming SECTIONS (Bates and Poole, 2003). In SECTIONS the 'S' stands for 'students' and includes student access to technology, and the 'E' relates to the ease of use. All other acronyms in ACTIONS remained the same. Each of the criteria for choosing the right blend of technologies relates to the following questions (Bates, 2005, pp. 49-50):

- Access: How accessible is a particular technology for learners? How flexible is it for a particular target group?
- Costs: What is the cost structure of each technology? What is the unit cost per student?
- Teaching and Learning: What kinds of learning are needed? What instructional approaches will best meet these needs? What are the best technologies supporting this teaching and learning?
- Interactivity and user-friendliness: What kind of interaction does this technology enable? How easy it is to use?

- Organizational issues: What are the organizational requirements, and the barriers to be removed, before this technology can be used successfully? What changes in organization need to be made?
- Novelty: How new is the technology?
- Speed: How quickly can courses be mounted with this technology? How quickly can materials be changed?

These criteria may be applied in choosing media for teaching any given topic. It is important to bear in mind that new technologies are not necessarily better than old ones. Simulations might be wonderful for the experimental sciences, but the cost of multi-media pre-prepared programs are very high ranging from tens to hundreds of thousands of dollars. Obviously, cost is a strong discriminator in the decision process of choosing between technologies. Some old technologies might be less expensive. It is also important to remember that the most important factor in teaching will always be the teacher. Bates states clearly that technology is not the issue. Good teaching is what matters most: "Good teaching may overcome a poor choice in the use of technology, but technology will never save bad teaching; usually it makes it worse" (Bates, 2005, p. 221). Obviously, teachers in any given subject matter, at various levels of education, have to decide what is the best combination of media that they prefer to use, and which media suit best their style of teaching and the available resources and infrastructure of the learning environment in which they teach.

Chapter 5

NAVIGATING BETWEEN CONTRASTING TRENDS

On top of the various problems which characterize the implementation efforts of the digital technologies in higher education settings, and that were discussed in the previous chapters, there are also general trends in higher education that affect macro-policy decisions as to what purposes should the new technologies be harnessed to promote. Higher education systems in the 21st century have been faced by most demanding challenges. Operating in a very complicated world, universities and other higher education institutions have to adjust themselves to handle concurrently contrasting trends (Barnett, 2000; Guri-Rosenblit et al., 2007; Weiler et al., 2008). They do not normally have the privilege of choosing either one or the other, but rather have to find a delicate and subtle balance between opposing policies. University leaders as well as policy makers of online ventures and technology initiatives have also to navigate between contrasting trends in defining the purpose and direction of their operation. This chapter examines the intricate and subtle interrelations between four pairs of contrasting trends which challenge higher education in general, and affect as well the implementation of the digital technologies in higher education settings: globalization versus national needs; broadening access versus marketization; competition versus collaboration; and intellectual property versus intellectual philanthropy.

GLOBALIZATION VERSUS NATIONAL NEEDS

The first medieval universities were quite international and global in their nature. Medieval scholars communicated in Latin and often studied and taught at several universities in different countries in Europe (Guri-Rosenblit, 2006). However, since the emergence of the nation states in the 19th century, universities served mainly nationalist ideas and interests. Universities of today are being challenged by globalization and internationalization trends. Some go so far to claim that the globalization process will give birth to a new grand model of a 'global university'. In his book on *The American Research University from World War II to World Wide Web,* Charles Vest, the former president of MIT, predicted that: "A global meta-university is arising that will accurately characterize higher education a decade or two hence in much the same way that Clark Kerr's multiversity accurately characterized American research universities forty years ago" (Vest, 2007, p. 108). In a special edition of the *Economist* which analyzed the state of art of higher education worldwide, it was claimed that: "Humboldt's university with its emphasis on research was one of the transformative institutions of the 19th century, the emerging global university is set to be one of the transformative institutions of the current era" (Economist, 2005d).

At the macro level, many higher education systems try to find today the optimal balance between operating in a global market and still focusing most of their endeavours catering to local and national priorities. Boundaries of what were relatively closed national systems are increasingly being penetrated by common international trends. It is often described as a process of opening closed or semi-closed markets for educational services. At the institutional level, many universities and colleges are torn nowadays between the growing pressure to operate in the global higher education market in order to diversify their funding base through various mechanisms, and their traditional roles of serving national priorities and accommodating mainly the needs of their local surrounding environments.

When the large scale distance teaching universities were established in the 1970s by national governments, for instance, their main operation was directed to absorb large numbers of students in their national jurisdictions (Guri-Rosenblit, 1999a,c). Only in the late 1990s, some of them, like the UK Open University, have started to expand their operation beyond their national boundaries, and this trend has intensified greatly in the last decade. A

Growing number of universities in the last decades have opened campuses and extensions around the world, and offer courses, diplomas and degrees fully online or in a blended model (Altbach and Balan, 2007; Barrow et al., 2003; Cohen, 2005; Douglass, 2005; Eckel and King, 2004; Economist, 2005b; Enders and Jongbloed, 2007; Mena, 2007; OECD, 2004). Unquestionably, the advent of the digital technologies has encouraged the expansion of globalized activities.

Ronald Robertson defined globalization as "a concept that refers to the compression of the world and the intensification of consciousness of the world as a whole" (Robertson, 1992, p. 8). Globalization is a multifaceted phenomenon, and it is manifested in economic, political and cultural dimensions. Whereas political, cultural and academic rationales have driven internationalization in the 1980s and 1990s, in the last decade economic rationales play a prominent role (van der Wende, 2001). The economic ideology of globalization that calls for the primacy of the market has become one of the defining features of higher education in the 21st century (Altbach, 2004; Barrow et al., 2003; Currie, 2005; Currie et al., 2003; Enders and Fulton 2002; van der Wende, 2002). The increasing pace and complexity of global knowledge flows, and the accelerating exchange of educational ideas, practices and policies, which have been facilitated by the abilities provided by the new technologies, constitute important drivers of globalization. Higher education is a key site for these flows and exchanges (Ninnes and Hellsten, 2005).

Changing recruitment markets for students and faculty reflect one of the major shifts in higher education policies. Higher education institutions in different countries are recruiting relatively new pools of students outside national borders. In this quest many are applying the new electronic technologies to expand enrollment, and to enhance the viability and profitability of international ventures. Douglass claims that the desire of institutions, either public or private, to increase international student enrollment constitutes a relatively new factor in higher education (Douglass, 2005). The motivations for this desire are multiple and are related to both economic and academic concerns (such as to increase the quality of the student pool). However, more and more, the motivation is to seek new revenue streams.

Transnational education is one of the potent manifestations of the impact of globalization upon higher education (Institutte of International Education,

2004). The number of transnational students worldwide, that either study abroad towards academic degrees or study within extensions of foreign universities in their own national jurisdiction, has increased dramatically in the last decade. According to OECD projections there will be around seven million transnational students in 2025 (Guri-Rosenblit et al., 2007). The positive aspects of transnational education include: widening of learning opportunities at various higher education levels by providing more choice for citizens in any given national jurisdiction; challenging traditional education systems by introducing more competition and innovative programs and delivery methods; helping make higher education more competitive; assisting in diversifying the budgeting of higher education; and benefiting through links with prestigious institutions, mainly in developing countries (UNESCO, 2003). However, there are also negative aspects of transnational education. Currently many unregulated providers of higher education operate for-profit in many countries. They are not subject to external or internal audit/monitoring processes, and their operation remains outside official national quality assurance regimes. Many of these institutions constitute 'degree mills' that provide low level education.

Globalization has different effects on differing regions, on different higher education systems and on various-type institutions (Douglass, 2005; Gibbons, 2003; Guri-Rosenblit, 2007; Rumble, 2001). It also encourages opposing trends. On one hand, globalization and the employment of the new technologies gave room for greater variety of non-traditional providers and niche players. On the other hand, noticeable efforts are being made internationally and nationally to converge and standardize undergraduate and graduate degree programs. This theme will be discussed further on in examining the contrasting trends of competition and collaboration in today's academic world.

In the wake of the globalization trends, a super model of world class universities has emerged as a unique and influential phenomenon. A special sub-set of studies has been developed to compare different league tables, with some countries and some institutions already headhunting for Nobel Prize laureates in order to improve their standing in some of the rankings (Altbach 2004; Altbach and Balan, 2007; European Commission, 2004; Weiler et al., 2008). The creation of 'world class universities' was spearheaded by the Ivy-league American universities, and to this date American universities dominate the prominent leagues tables, such as the Shanghai Ranking of the Jio-Tong

University. In an article in the *Economist* on the growing market-oriented higher education, the global world class universities were defined as "citizens of a global economy, sending their best graduates to work for multinational companies" (Economist, 2005d). This article also emphasized that global universities do not have to have necessarily a physical presence abroad to be worthy of the name. Some of the world's best universities have been reluctant to set up campuses abroad, and some of the most enthusiastic off-shores, are hardly global in the sense of having world class faculty and the pick of the world's graduate students.

Many governments around the world are obsessed at present with establishing world class universities. The British have introduced fees in part because they want their best universities to be able to compete with the best American ones. The German Social Democratic Party, traditionally a bastion of egalitarianism, has produced a plan to create German equivalents of Harvard, Princeton and Stanford. Three such universities, out of more than 300 universities in Germany, were selected in 2007 and are going to get most generous funds from the federal German government to enhance their research infrastrúcture and their global standing. Policy makers in China and India are hard at work trying to build world class universities, denoting to such enterprises huge amounts of money (Altbach and Balan, 2007; Economist, 2005d).

Some of the leading world class universities have also produced huge economic benefits in participating in the development of advanced and sophisticated technologies. Stanford University helped to incubate Google, Yahoo, Cisco, Sun Microsystems and many other world-changing firms. The University of Texas at Austin has helped to create a high-technology cluster that employed in 2003 around 100,000 people in some 1,700 companies. In 2000, the eight research universities in Boston provided a $7.4 billion boost to the region's economy, generated 264 new patents and granted 280 licenses to private enterprises (Economist, 2005d). In other words, leading research universities in the US have not only been assisted by the digital technologies to spread their influence globalwide, but they have actually participated in developing most the advanced technological innovations and infrastructures in the last decades, and continue being engaged in generating new advanced technological devices and platforms.

Some claim that the growing importance attached to the leading world class universities, have pushed many countries to divert special resources to establish such universities of their own, and diminish their investment in other higher education institutions. By doing so, they have harmed the development of their higher education systems at large. Ordorika argued passionately that globalization trends, while facilitating networking, collaboration, and flexibility between systems, also threaten the stability, security and identity of universities in some national settings (Ordorika, 2006). He argued that if a country like Mexico will devote lots of efforts and great amounts of budgeting in trying to establish a 'world class university', it will be destructive and harmful for the overall higher education system in Mexico. There are many urgent national needs which higher education systems in countries, like Mexico, have to achieve, and establishing a 'world class university' is not one of them.

It is of tremendous importance to pay careful attention to the advantages of globalization trends in national higher education settings. There are acute differences between developing and developed countries, and between different-type higher education institutions within any given country. Some universities are much more generously endowed and equipped to serve a broader range of functions in a global context, even beyond the needs of their particular environment and society, while many others need to concentrate first and foremost on the present and future knowledge needs of their own communities, and develop their special loci of expertise (Neave, 2000; Ordorika, 2006; Weiler et al., 2008). Most of the developing countries should focus most of their efforts to strengthen their national infrastructures.

A growing body of case studies point to the complexity of globalization in influencing the future of higher education. Douglass (2005) claims that in effect, all globalization is local, in the sense that each academic environment reacts to the globalization trends in a unique way which reflects the dominant academic culture in each setting. Delineating the experience and responses of differing institutions may help us more readily to understand the true influence of globalization and the future path for higher education at various places. Ninnes and Hellsten (2005) in their book on *Internationalizing Higher Education: Critical Explorations of Pedagogy and Policy* cast a critical eye on the internationalization of higher education. They peel back taken-for-granted practices and beliefs, and address the ambiguities, tensions and contradictions in internationalization. Scholars from a range of disciplines and regions critically examine the co-modification of higher education, and the many problems which are still associated with support for international students, international partnerships for aid and trade, and the impacts on academics' work.

One of the few certainties in the global higher education market is the presence of continual change and changing expectations. Douglass claims that permanence and stability will become less important in higher education systems than flexibility and creativity (Douglass, 2005). Considering that we cannot eliminate globalization trends, even if we do not like some of their results, we have to adjust to them and see what can be gained from them, while at the same time taking care of the national contexts (Weiler et al., 2008).

BROADENING ACCESS VERSUS MARKETIZATION

The new technologies, by their very nature, open up the possibilities of widening access to higher education for new student clienteles both in developing and developed countries, and by doing so they promote social equity (Gladieux and Swail, 1999; Guri-Rosenblit, 2007; Shearer and Chakiris, 2006). New potential student constituencies include different groups. One such group consists of adults studying for recreational purposes, who are willing to pursue fields of study different from those of their professional careers. Another large group of new student clienteles are professionals willing to upgrade their professional knowledge and expertise on an ongoing basis. As aforementioned in Chapter 4, the most successful e-learning ventures take place in professional training and professional upgrade programs (Adelman, 2000; Arafeh, 2004; Blumenstyk, 2003; Matkin, 2002; Ryan, 2002; Trucano, 2005). Many students in the future are likely to study while they work. Being highly mobile, they will expect to continue studying while they move between different national boundaries, and e-learning will constitute an important tool for achieving this purpose in the growing entrepreneurial and globalized economies (Barrow et al., 2003; Clark, 1998; Enders and Fulton, 2002; Enders and Jongbloed, 2007; Mitrano, 2006; OECD, 2005).

As discussed earlier in Chapter 1, a large group of students who study in distance teaching frameworks, offered online or through other media, are defined as 'second-chancers' for a variety of reasons. Many of the second-chance students, that have no sufficient entry requirements to conventional universities, are usually less qualified to study independently, and are unprepared to cope with academic study. The accumulated experience of the large distance teaching universities indicates clearly that in order to deal effectively with second-chance, unprepared students, it is crucially important to back the teaching/learning processes with efficient delivery and support systems (Tait and Mills, 2003; Brindley et al., 2004; Guri-Rosenblit, 2005a,b). Many of the distance teaching universities provide their students with occasional campus-like grounds within regional and local study centers to meet and interact with each other, summer residential schools, personal tutors, professional counselors and intensive tutorials.

Undoubtedly, unprepared and less qualified students are less qualified to use the new technologies' capabilities without an intensive and steady support. Sir John Daniel, who served until 2001 as the Vice-Chancellor of the UK Open University, stressed already in 1996 that the potential success of the innovative electronic technologies depends to a great extent on the ability to provide individual learners with adequate backup throughout their studies. Daniel asked: "Can we through electronic mail, computer conferencing and the World Wide Web, provide the level of individual student support that we think necessary? We are experimenting with that, but despite all the arm waving, I think the jury is still out. If the jury comes back and declares us guilty of being able to provide effective, personal, tutorial support to students on a large scale, then all sorts of things become possible" (Daniel 1996, p. 38).

It seems that since Daniel had phrased this question, the jury has raised its verdict - such support is possible when teaching online very small numbers of students, and such mode of teaching is most costly. This fact explains why most successful e-learning programs take place at the graduate, post-graduate and professional training levels. Undergraduate students, and particularly weak students, need a lot of support and reinforcement both in regular and virtual classes. They cannot benefit from the wide plethora of programs put currently on the Internet without constant support and a caring and supportive environment (Brindley et. al., 2004; Hulsmann, 2004; Institute for Higher Educatin Policy, 2000; Porter and O'Connor, 2001; Tait and Mills, 2003). In other words, the potential of the new technologies to widen access to large numbers of young and unprepared students, both in developed and in developing countries, is most limited in reality. In sum, it can be concluded that the digital technologies have the potential to attract new student clienteles, and thus contribute both to access and equity in higher education, but at a much slower pace as initially has been previously anticipated.

Side by side with expanding their higher education systems, a growing number of countries are trying to turn higher education into export industries. Whatever its actual influence, there is a general sense that GATS (General Agreement of Trade in Services) reflects a shift in how nation-states may view higher education. Green (2004) stated that:"Liberalization of trade in education may weaken government's commitment to and investment in public higher education, promote privatization, and put countries with weak quality assurance mechanisms at a disadvantage in their countries by foreign providers" (in Douglass, 2005, p. 7). Most of those who are negotiating the GATS agreement are not members of the higher education community, rather they are government officials concerned about opening markets and promoting trade - whether it be educational services or steel. The decline in traditional resources in the midst of growing public demand for higher education has been accompanied by a rise in competition from new higher providers, some local and some global, and in a shift in the dynamic of competition for students.

UK is currently one of the leading exporters of higher education. According to the Shanghai Ranking of Higher Education Institutions, the UK has the second largest global market share, (behind the US), which is worth up to £11 billion directly and £12 billion indirectly to the UK economy each year. Many of the UK universities are international in their nature with long-established links with universities and other organizations around the world. They have been consistently successful in welcoming international students and researchers attracted by the wide range of high quality courses and educational support, and a world class research base. In 2003/04 there were 213,000 international students and 104,000 students from other EU countries in UK higher education institutions. There are also many more international and EU students on exchange (Socrates-Erasmus) and study-abroad programs in extensions of UK universities (Eggins, 2006).

This marketization orientation of the UK higher education in the last decades constitutes a huge shift from the long standing academic culture in English universities, which are mostly public universities (except Buckingham University which is a tiny private university). English universities (not the Scottish ones) for centuries "often spiced de-facto elitism with anti-business snobbery" (Economist, 2005d). Less than fifty years ago, many of the English universities were not just reluctant to be regarded as 'knowledge producers', they were antagonistic to the capitalist market economy, at large. Oxford and

Cambridge, for instance, long resisted the study of practical subjects such as business or engineering; "instead, they specialized in turning the sons of businessmen into educated gentlemen. This anti-business bias reached its apogee in the 1960s, when many of the current generation of dons got their jobs" (ibid).

The emergence of the World Wide Web and the globalization of higher education have introduced a profound change in the dominant British culture. Cambridge University, for instance, could not have resisted the generous offer of Microsoft in 1997 to establish a joint venture between Microsoft Research Ltd. and the computer science lab of Cambridge University. Microsoft invested then $80 million for a period of five years. "It's valuable to have a diversity of opinion when you are trying to solve problems no one has ever solved before" was the reason provided by Nathan Myhrvold, Microsoft's chief technology officer then, for the decision of Microsoft to establish research labs both at MIT in the US and at Cambridge University in the UK (Grossman, 1997). Cambridge had in 1997 already joint ventures with some other business corporations, like Olivetti and Xerox. Unquestionably, the emergence of the Internet and the enhancement of the global market have prompted the UK universities to become more market-oriented. Now the UK is one of the leading countries in the marketization of higher education.

The leader of higher education export and marketization is USA. Many American respectable and well established universities have initiated in the last decade new study tracks for profit generation. Harvard, Dartmouth, John Hopkins and Brown universities, for instance, have been investing in recent years in for-profit college companies (Blumenstyk, 2003). Some of the programs that the for-profit companies offer have nothing in common with the traditional core curricula of these elite research universities. Harvard University, for example, is the biggest institutional investor in a $590 million fund run by Boston's Charlesbank Capital partners, which made its foray into the sector in April 2002 by investing in a school that trains automobile and motorcycle technicians (ibid) - not exactly typical Harvard students.

Many of the for-profit ventures of some leading universities in the US have failed. Over the past decade there was a strong sense in American universities of a largely untapped market for online programs and a strong belief in the ability of brand name universities to enter major and developing international markets (Allen and Seaman, 2003). One of the apparent lessons of the last decade is that there is indeed a growing market for online courses and degree programs, but the market is narrower than previously predicted. Only a few ventures captured the student market they had hoped for. Many of the American ventures have experienced limited success internationally. It turned out that they have overextended and overestimated the market demand in such places as China and Malaysia. Many for-profit ventures that had been initiated in the last decade by leading universities in the US, and were targeted mainly to domestic students, have failed as well. Some examples are outlined below.

One of the most adventurous and highly funded projects involving top universities, including the University of Chicago and Columbia University - UNext.com, has eaten up $200 million within a two year period, with little or no prospect of return for investors (Matkin, 2002). In its two year operation the venture featured materials from a dozen prominent institutions and attracted a widespread media attention, but it was never profitable. It suffered many critics from the Columbia faculty because of the losses it has sustained. UNext was obliged to redefine its initial target audience and reduce significantly its anticipated revenues.

Fathom Knowledge Network Inc., another initiative of Columbia University, has failed also after a few years. Under the premise that universities are entrepreneurs who could sell their intellectual capital and get a high revenue for doing it, Columbia University set out to establish a for-profit unit in 1999. Fathom Knowledge Network Inc. was designed as a portal for courses and e-learning materials developed by Columbia and 13 other universities, libraries and museums. Early partners included the University of Chicago, Cambridge University Press, and the New York Library. Fathom began with a $20 million investment by partners, growing to some $200 million. Fathom projected 200,000 registered users within 18 months, with about 20,000 paying students registered in Fathom courses. But after nearly two years, it could count only a few hundred paying students, and it closed down after raising revenues of only $700,000 (Carlson, 2003b).

Some additional failures have been dramatic with dire consequences to several universities. High profile failures include NYUOnline that launched in 1999 a for-profit arm. NYUonline set out to capture a seemingly lucrative corporate-education service, banking on its name recognition to create an instant market. After three years it announced that it will close as a separate division of NYU, fold some of its operations back into the School of Continuing and Professional Education, and sell its infrastructure. NYU had invested $21.5 million into NYUOnline by July 2001 (Ryan, 2002). The respected Temple University had abandoned Virtual Temple in July 2001 without offering a single course (Blumenstyk, 2001). Jones International University with the backing of the multi-millionaire Glenn Jones and the Apollo Group, has not performed to its initial expectations. It attracted only 200 degree students by mid 2001, and graduated only 10 students in total, in 2001 (ibid).

A number of other consortia involving public universities have suffered similar difficulties (Matkin, 2002; McKenzie, 20023; Ryan, 2002; Washburn, 2005). Caliber, the Wharton School's e-partner, filed for bankruptcy after a short period of operation. Also California Virtual University failed. It was established as a portal to a rather sparse number of online courses offered by member public Californian universities. Here too, enrollment numbers were well below projections in the initial years of the venture. With the decline in the economy, California Virtual University has been closed.

Not only American ventures suffered a blow. The UKeU (UK e-Learning University) provides an example of a huge failure. It was initiated by the British government with an initial government investment of £62 million. UKeU hired business managers in nine countries and acquired 26 local higher education partners in six countries. But shortly after opening its business in March 2003, UKeU looked like a bust. Enrollment levels were dismal. Only 900 students had enrolled in online courses, well below the 5,000 student target. In March 2004 the chief executive of the Higher Education Funding Council of England, Sir Harold Newby, announced the demise of the UKeU. He provided two reasons for the failure: one was the preference of students and partner universities for blended courses, and another was a sense that the venture poured most of its resources in the UKeU web-based platform and little into actual course content (Garret, 2004b).

Nevertheless, though many university ventures of online education and training had suffered spectacular failures, it is not sufficient to doubt the entire e-learning enterprise. Early failures should be expected in any new undertaking, as successful models sort themselves out from unsuccessful ones. The new technologies still hold a huge promise for attracting new student clienteles to higher education, both in developed and in developing countries. Obviously, the transition to a more market-oriented system in higher education is not easy and entails numerous obstacles. Countries will have to cope with a host of new problems that come along with newly liberated markets: They will have to solve problems associated with social justice and equity, regulation of foreign universities, differences in national standards, how to prevent outright cheating, such as selling degrees, how to set efficient national and international quality assurance mechanisms, etc.

COMPETITION VERSUS COLLABORATION

Another pair of contrasting trends relates to the conflicting world in which higher education institutions are required to both compete and collaborate with their counterparts. On the one hand, they are told to thrive and develop through competition and become more and more entrepreneurial in diversifying their funding base. On the other hand, they are being told to collaborate with one another, and strengthen their standing through partnering with beneficial and worthwhile partners. It is quite clear that, in the world of higher education, as elsewhere, one cannot avoid competition for scarce resources, be it research funding, good faculty or good students. At the same time, successful collaborative ventures hold great potential for generating additional resources and recruiting new student clienteles (Guri-Rosenblit, 2007; Todd and Edmonds, 2006; Vincent-Lancrin, 2004; Weiler et al., 2008). Many international bodies encourage, and even condition funding of research projects by forcing collaboration between several higher education institutions, preferably from different countries. An influential norm in the research domain is reflected in a growing trend of forming interdisciplinary teams within and across institutions. Each higher education institution has to define today both its competing parties and its potential collaborators.

Adrian Wooldridge, Washington Bureau Chief of *Economist* in a comprehensive survey conducted on higher education worldwide and published on September 8th, 2005, concluded that the massification of higher education and the continuous decline in government budgeting in the last decades have forced universities all over the world to become more diverse, more global and more competitive (Economist, 2005b). As a matter fact the overall expenditure on higher education has increased in most countries in the last decades, but since the participation rate in higher education has grown dramatically, and so has the number and variety of higher education institutions, a substantial decline in the funding of each institution took place.

Many universities and colleges are forced today to generate new revenue streams.

The digital technologies have contributed to a growing competitive environment between existing and new higher education providers, including a rise of new non-traditional and for-profit competitors. The rise of these new competitors is being facilitated by the movement of national governments to deregulate their higher education sectors, providing new levels of autonomy for institutions to become more entrepreneurial in their institutional policies (Clark, 1998). Douglass argued the new technologies have introduced into the world of higher education a 'new Darwinian environment' in which many old and new institutions will learn to adopt the advanced technologies for their purposes and thrive, while many others will perish (Douglass, 2005).

Some of the new providers have a competitive advantage over the traditional institutions, in large part because they do not have to restructure existing infrastructures, but rather base their operation from the start on the grounds of innovative platforms. The large scale distance teaching universities which are based on the industrial model provide a good example of the difficulties that some higher education institutions face in their attempt to employ the new technologies. As discussed earlier in Chapter 4, these universities find it most difficult to adopt the information and communication technologies on a broad institutional level, since in order to so, they have to restructure drastically their overall infrastructures and underlying premises. The industrial model of distance education is based on totally different underlying principles as compared to online teaching. New online ventures did not have to restructure any existent infrastructures. From the outset they have built their operation on the new infrastructures developed for learning and teaching online.

There are three major strategies that higher education institutions can adopt in responding to the growing competition: to strengthen their relative advantages and demonstrate excellence in specific areas; to collaborate with other competing institutions in an attempt to reduce the competitive risk; and to extend their operation beyond local and national boundaries to international markets.

Partnerships, if they are successful, create greater strengths. The basic underlying idea behind cooperation is that the *whole* may be greater than the *sum of its parts*. The synergy that comes from collaboration can often yield benefits well beyond those originally envisioned. Failure to collaborate results often in an unnecessary duplication of effort and in ineffective investments of scarce resources. But the fact is that successful collaborations are immensely difficult to achieve and sustain. Many failures are reported in the relevant literature. Many collaborative ventures turn to be more fanfare than reality, and those that have been implemented successfully did not always turn out as intended. In fact, most collaborations produce something different from the originally stated goals, sometimes for the better, and sometimes for the worse.

Clearly, there are significant differences in cultures of various organizations which render the management of collaborative ventures extremely difficult. Collaboration requires an unusual degree of self-confidence and openness, but the rewards can be considerable if the fit between the participating institutions is a good one. For a collaboration to succeed it is important to: accommodate institutional cultures; build trust relations and perceive mutual benefits. Paul, humorously, reached an interesting insight as to the deteriorating intensity of cooperation as it moves from top-down decisions to the practical, operational levels: "Inter-institutional agreement is more likely the higher one goes in the organization. Hence, presidents will agree almost on anything with each other, vice-presidents will usually find a way through, while deans are much more skeptical. Faculty are strongly resistant, and academic secretaries don't want to know" (Paul, 1990, p. 148).

Interestingly, the competitive global markets of higher education have encouraged a growing trend of collaboration between many nations in an attempt to define international accreditation processes and establish effective quality procedures. International recognition and collaboration in research has long been the ultimate standard for assessing the research and scholarly quality of individual faculty and academic departments. But currently the international collaboration has moved to agreements related to the evaluation of teaching and academic diplomas.

Throughout the European Union, for instance, there is a growing evidence of cross-national cooperation in educational credentialing, despite long traditions of institutional autonomy in most European countries. Bologna Process provides the most impressive collaborative venture signed currently by 46 countries, mostly from Europe, but also some outside Europe, like Armenia, Azerbaijan and Georgia.

The Bologna Agreement provides and example of an international framework that is pushing for convergence among various degree patterns offered by European universities. The Bologna Process that has started in Europe in 1999 is a macro level attempt to harmonize the European higher education systems, and to coordinate the huge diversity of higher education organizational structures (Guri-Rosenblit et al., 2007).

National systems of higher education have long been characterized by significant differences in the organization of secondary schools, in qualifications for university enrolment, in the requirements for various degree programs and time to completion, and in administrative structures. The Bologna agreement marks a significant attempt at convergence, in part to facilitate cross-border articulation of degree requirements, as well as to help foster a greater international flow of students and scholarly activity. Those institutions and national systems that do move towards convergence, particularly in degree requirements, will be significantly more competitive internationally.

There is both a need and a significant trend among many national governments to adopt multinational agreements on higher education reforms, and to seek achieve restructuring of academic programs. The North American Free Trade Agreement (NAFTA) signed between USA, Canada an Mexico in 1993 provides an example of a regional consortium that aims to compete against comparable trading blocs centered in Japan and the European Union (Barrow et al., 2003). Higher education constitutes an important commodity in NAFTA. The operation of NAFTA highlights the fact that cooperation and competition are strongly interwoven. Most collaborative ventures are created in order to compete against other entities.

As mentioned earlier, many collaborative ventures have been forged in the last decade between universities and the private sector. The formation of the Higher Education Leadership Forum provides an interesting example of collaboration between a research company and a leading academic publication. The *Higher Education Chronicle*, which is the leading news source in US higher education, joined forces on October 2005 with the Gartner Company, which is one of the largest and most trusted independent companies for research and analysis of the information technologies, with more than 1,200 analysts worldwide, and more than 10,000 annual client engagements (Economist, 2005c). This joint venture intended "to bring together top academic leaders from the world of technology for the first time ever to discuss the key issues that colleges and universities face" (ibid). Undoubtedly, the Leadership Forum has undertook a most important endevour for discussing the future of higher education and analyzing how the new technologies will shape this future.

INTELLECTUAL PROPERTY VERSUS INTELLECTUAL PHILANTHROPY

The preservation of the intellectual property of academics' research and a growing trend of academic philanthropy constitute an interesting pair of contrasting trends. Both trends have been enhanced by the knowledge revolution through the emergence of the digital technologies. Many countries have defined in the last decade stringent copyright regulations and invested great efforts in registering patents. A new 'cyber law' field has been born to deal with intellectual property issues in the Internet. At the same time an intriguing movement has started to evolve advocating open source policies, and this movement is gaining momentum in an accelerated pace.

The Intellectual Property domain includes several areas: copyright, patents, trademarks, industrial design rights, utility models, and so on. Relevant to the academic world are mainly patents and copyright. Copyright laws cover the creative or artistic expression of ideas, while patent laws cover inventions. A patent is a set of exclusive rights granted by a state to an inventor for a fixed period of time in exchange for a disclosure of the invention. The patent is not a right to use or practice the invention, but it rather provides the right to exclude others from making, using, selling, offering for sale, or importing the patented invention for the term of the patent which is usually twenty years from the filing date. There are complicated (and quite often expensive) regulations that set the norms for getting a patent right. Many hard science inventions, in fields of biotechnology, nanotechnology and pharmacology are most active in registering patents. In the last decades, various collaborations between universities and the corporate world have led to disputes over patenting, some of which ended at the court.

The most problematic area of widespread violations of academic work, enhanced greatly by the new technologies, relates to copyright. Gantz and Rochester entitled the phenomenon of violating academic copyrights on books, publication and other research artifacts as the 'Pirates of the Digital Millennium' (Gantz and Rochester, 2005). 'Copyright' is a legal concept, enacted by governments, giving the creator of an original work of authorship exclusive rights to it, usually for a limited time (of fifty to hundred years) after which the work enters the public domain. The copyright privileges also give the copyright holder the right to be accredited for the work, to determine who may adapt the work to other forms, who may perform the work, who may financially benefit from it, and other related rights.

Most countries recognize copyright limitations, allowing 'fair use' exceptions to the creators exclusivity of copyright and giving users certain rights. The development of the Internet, the digital media and the computer networked technologies, have introduced numerous difficulties in enforcing copyright and prompted a reinterpretation of the meaning of 'fair use' in online teaching. Simultaneously, academic publishing houses, which depend to a great extent on copyright have advocated the extension and expansion of their copyright, and filed for stringent legal reinforcement (Dowd, 2006; Dupin-Bryant, 2006; Lindsey, 2003). Publishers and other content owners express fear that expanded exemptions for digital materials used in online learning will adversely affect the viability of their business. They fear that the digital content released in an educational setting will be widely redistributed by students. Some of the publishing houses hold a view that educators "want something for nothing" (Tanner, 1999).

Copyright laws in most countries do not prohibit all copying and replication. In the US, the fair use doctrine, codified by the Copyright Act of 1976, permits some copying and distribution without needing permission of the copyright holder or payment to him. The statute does not clearly define fair use, but instead defines four factors to consider in judging fair use: (1) The purpose and character of the use; (2) the nature of the copyrighted work; (3) the amount and substantiality of the portion used in relation to the copyrighted work as a whole; and (4) the effect of the use upon the potential market of the copyrighted work. Later legal acts amended the US Copyright law so that for certain purposes making 10 copies or more is construed to be commercial. The Digital Millennium Copyright Act prohibits the manufacture, importation, or distribution of devices whose intended use is to bypass an access or copy control put in place by a copyright owner.

Academics confront several dilemmas in relation to copyright laws in the digital millennium. On one hand, they are concerned as to losing intellectual property over their course materials, some of which include innovative ideas and original constructs. On the other hand, the stringent copyright laws initiated and formulated in the last decade as to the use of others' works in their ongoing teaching, as they do regularly in classroom teaching, might deter them from utilizing the new technologies in their teaching.

Michael Tanner, a professor of computer science in the School of Engineering at the University of California in Santa Cruz, that was quoted earlier in Chapter 2 on the issue of fair use of materials in online teaching, argued in favour of expanding the copyright law's existing exemptions for education. The great opportunities offered by the Internet for higher education requires that the exemptions currently offered for classroom teaching be extended to the networked environment. Tanner claimed that the publishing houses should not worry of losing their financial base, since academic faculty and institutions alike have strong interests in controlling who has access to online classes. The more interactivity is built into an online resource, the more care is given to protect the privacy of participants. The general public is usually not offered free access to online classes, if it is not intended to be an open source, as discussed further on.

Tanner claimed in 1999 in his testimony before the Representatives of the US Copyright Office that: "We can assure copyright owners that material made available through educational exemptions will be contained within a limited community. We will cooperate with and respect limitations on copying and distribution. However, if such cooperation is unreasonably burdensome or intrusive, faculty will frequently choose not to use the material in question. Already, anxiety is high in academia about the kind of demands proprietors will make in exchange for allowing their copyrighted material to be transmitted to students over networks. Stories of exorbitant prices and intrusive technologies that track individual use of copyrighted works distract and alarm faculty whose primary interest is in sharing knowledge and understanding with their students" (Tanner, 1999).

Tanner proposed to distinguish between two kinds of protection that must be in place to ensure that copyrighted material used under exemptions does not go into general circulation. First, measures need to be in place to ensure limited access, so that the transmitted material is available only to authorized users, such as students enrolled in a class. Second, it must be possible to prevent permanent storage and redistribution of the material. Various models of access control technology are already in the market, and others are under development. These include both hardware and software approaches and range from strong encryption to weak protections based on passwords and IP addresses. Determined assault should be deterred by criminal penalties.

Side by side with the ongoing discussions and actions in the last decade, both legal and public, on issues related to copyright in the academic world, an intriguing movement of open sources has emerged (Carmichael and Honour, 2002; Wong and Sayo, 2004). Clearly, more open access to sources of scholarly information, libraries, and software codes benefit all participants in higher education, but most particularly it benefits teaching and research in those countries that suffer from severe shortages in adequate academic manpower and research facilities. The MIT's Open Courseware Project was one of the pioneers in promoting open source materials (Olsen, 2002; Vest, 2001, 2007). By fall 2006, about 80% of MIT's academic faculty had mounted materials of about 1,550 subjects from 39 academic disciplines (Vest, 2007, p. 97). The Open Courseware site averages more than one million visits per month. Visitors are located on every continent: "Forty-three percent of the traffic is from North America, 20% from East Asia, and 16% from Western Europe. The remaining 20% of users are distributed across Latin America, Eastern Europe, the Middle East, the Pacific Region, and Sub-Saharan Africa" (ibid, pp. 97-98).

Charles Vest, who presided over MIT from1990 until 2004, when the Open Courseware Project was initiated, highlights the immense importance of 'intellectual philanthropy': "Open Courseware seems counterintuitive in a market-driven world, but it represents the intellectual generosity that faculties of great American universities have demonstrated in many ways over the years. In an innovative manner, it expresses a belief that education can be advanced around the world by constantly widening access to information and pedagogical organization, and by inspiring others to participate" (ibid, 98).

Today, the open source movement is a wide-ranging phenomenon (Biltzer and Schroder, 2006). Before the term 'open source' became widely adopted, developers and producers used a variety of phrases to describe the concept of practical accessibility to a product's source. Interestingly, the birth of the Internet in 1969 was a product of a collaborative process used by researchers with access to the Advanced Research Projects Agency to develop telecommunication network protocols. Essentially born out of a desire for increased general access to digital media, the Internet is in effect the most prominent open source medium.

The rise of open source culture in the last decade emerged as a counter-hegemony to the increasingly restrictive intellectual property laws and policies governing access to copyrighted content. The underlying premise of the

Creative Commons (CC) movement is antithetical to the Copyright © idea. The extensions to the term of copyright, such as those articulated in the Digital Millennium Copyright Act in the US have created a 'chilling effect' among many cultural practitioners and academic faculty.

Achieving the goal of making cultural or academic work widely available has been enabled by the digital media. The explosive growth in personal computers ownership resulted in a dramatic increase in the general population's access to digital media. Artists and users who choose to distribute their work digitally face none of the physical limitations that traditional cultural producers have been typically faced with.

Within the academic community there are currently many initiatives widening the open source usage all over the world (Weiler et al., 2008). Many higher education institutions create open source infrastructures following the MIT Open Courseware initiative (Gourley, 2008). Such open source frameworks enable to access instructional resources and academic courses in a plethora of areas. Another area in which the open source in academia flourishes relates to research products. Many funded research products are put available on the Internet. One of the most influential initiatives in the open source movement took place in academic publishing. There are currently a handful of open access journals where full-text articles are available for free online. Still, most of the journals publish just the abstracts of the articles, and charge a fee, either to individual users or to libraries, to access the full texts. The venerable National Institute for Health (NIH) in the US has proposed in 2007 a policy on 'Enhanced Public Access to NIH Research Information'. This policy would provide a free, searchable source for NIH-funded results to the public six months after its initial publication. The underlying reason for this move is that since a significant amount of public funding budgets the NIH research operations, the products of research should be open to the public.

Organizations like OECD, the World Bank and UNESCO, have joined in the last decade the effort to make their influence felt in the direction of advancing the development of the open source movement, making vital resources of research and teaching more openly and equitably available, to the benefit of all, and particularly to developing countries. It is most likely that the openness and sharing of intellectual resources in the academic world will grow immensely in the near future, and will enhance the globalization of higher education.

Chapter 6

Quo Vadis? – Some Future Trends

Sir Arthur Clarke has phrased a most illuminating insight as to the adoption cycle of new technologies by the human mankind: "When it comes to technology, most people overestimate it in the short term and underestimate it in the long term" (in Twigg, 2004). This insight seems to hold true for the implementation of the digital technologies in higher education settings. Peter Drucker strongly believed that it is possible "to identify and prepare for the future that has already happened" (Drucker, 1998, p. 16), and when interviewed for the Forbes magazine in 1997 he firmly stated that: "Thirty years from now the big university campuses will be relics. Universities won't survive. It's as large a change as when we first got the printed book" (Drucker, 1997). Quite clearly, this prediction about the demise of the old university structure seems nowadays as a sweeping exaggeration that "dates back to a period of a naive optimism", as Visser defined it (Visser, 2006, p. 193), about the expected impacts of the Internet. We have seen since then that many of the expectations prevalent at the 1990s about the huge impacts of the new technologies on higher education have remained unfulfilled. The supremacy of the campuses has not been threatened so far by the electronic media, nor has the academic culture been changed in fundamental ways, as some might have predicted earlier. Many researchers and policy makers debate as to what is going to be the future of the digital media in higher education settings - "Is it going to be a sunrise or a perfect storm?" as Hilton phrased it (Hilton, 2006).

Some scholars believe that the advanced technologies are going to affect more deeply the three major elements of scholarly activity: the creation of information, the preservation of information, and the transmission of information (Noam, 1999; Pfeffer, 2003). Wilson stated that: "The e-learning revolution is not over. It is just entering a more intelligent and less self-indulgent phase" (Wilson, 2002, p. 5). Noble claimed that the story of e-learning is still unfolding, no one really knows what tomorrow will bring (Noble, 2001). Wilson and Noble echo the beliefs of many other researchers as to the future potential of the advanced technologies in higher education.

Based on many predictions in the vast literature dealing with the multiple impacts of the digital media in higher education, we sum up below the most noticeable future trends that are likely to take place, following a deeper penetration of the advanced technologies into various layers of the academic world.

PROMOTING INSTITUTIONAL DIVERSITY

One of the defining features of higher education systems in the last fifty years is the growing diversity of institutions. Different-type institutions were established to accommodate the growing demand for higher education and the diverse needs and abilities of heterogeneous student clienteles and emerging new professions. By 2006 there were approximately 140 million students all over the world studying in higher education institutions, representing about 20% of the relevant age cohort, whereas at the start of the 20th century only about 500,000 students were enrolled in universities worldwide. In some of the developed countries the participation rate of the relevant age cohort in higher education has reached over 50% (Clancy et al., 2007). The employment of the advanced technologies has enhanced the diversity in higher education by providing more alternative forms for organizing teaching, learning and scholarship, and by attracting new student cohorts to enroll at various-type higher education institutions. Virtual universities, corporate universities, off-shore operations, various forms of distance education, online education and self-paced learning are likely to grow in the future.

Beaudoin predicted that in the US higher education: "We are likely to see a major shift occurring in the next 10 to 15 years in the composition and structure of our educational institutions. There will be fewer residential colleges, although most will remain to provide younger students with the traditional trappings of a campus experience. There will be an expanding continuing education and training sector delivered by employers and companies outside academe. In fact, these for-profits are already working under contract with many colleges to provide various academic and non-academic services. Another major component is the expanding electronic campus whereby students can access learning opportunities via computer from home, work, dorm, community, or other locations, whenever it is convenient" (Beaudoin, 2006b, p. 5). Vest envisioned that though campuses will always stay important in the academic world "they will do so on a digital platform of shared information, materials, and experience that will raise quality and access all around' (Vest, 2007, p. 109).

Interestingly, in spite of all these changes that are likely to occur in the near future, Beaudoin believes that altogether they will have a little fundamental impact on higher education establishments (Beaudoin, 2006b). Despite external forces that will challenge the educational sector, as well as present it with new opportunities, internal resistance will stubbornly preserve much of the dominant culture that now prevails. Many studies and wide range reviews on the applications of the digital technologies in higher education reflect a general agreement that the new technologies are not likely to endanger the existence of conventional campus universities, but rather enrich, support and enhance many of their activities (Arafeh, 2004; Bates, 2001, 2005, 2007; Boezerooij, 2006; 1999; Collis and Moonen, 2001; Donnelly and McSweeney, 2008; Harper et al., 2000; Harley et al., 2002; OECD, 2005; Trucano, 2005; Van der Wende, 2002).

Universities, colleges and other higher education institutions that utilize the digital technologies vary enormously in how they were initiated, the clienteles they aim to serve, how they are funded, and the kinds of programs they offer. Consortia-type ventures constitute a leading model in the last decades. A number of universities join forces, either within national higher education systems or as an international enterprise, to offer a variety of programs either by establishing physical extensions at various locations, or offering their programs fully online or in a blended mode. Many university consortia do operate in European countries, such as Norway, Sweden, Finland, Denmark, Italy (CHEPS, 2002; Collis and Moonen, 2001; Hanna, 2003; Van der Molen, 2001; UNESCO, 2005). Many new consortia have been formed in the last decade between universities across oceans, such as a consortium that was established between English, Canadian and Australian universities to offer business administration programs in Vietnam (Guri-Rosenblit, 2005b). Many of the consortia partnerships were created between universities and the corporate world, as discussed earlier in Chapters 4 and 5. The consortium model has been greatly enhanced by the digital technologies. In spite of the many failures that were reported and discussed earlier, consortia-type ventures are likely to proliferate in the future.

Dual-mode universities constitute an additional leading model in current online education provision. Before the emergence of the new technologies, this model has been activated mainly in Australia and in Canada, as well as in several Eastern European countries (Evans and Nation, 2000; Guri-Rosenblit, 1999a). Dual-mode universities teach simultaneously on-campus and off-campus students, and the same admission requirements apply to both categories of students. The underlying idea behind the dual-mode model is that the same curricula can be offered to both on- and off-campus students through appropriate channels of communication. Evidently, the new information and communication technologies facilitate the provision of courses to distant students, and enable an ongoing interaction with them in the study process. The new technologies have actually turned the dual-mode provision into a leading model in most higher education systems worldwide, as many conventional universities decided to adopt them for offering various forms of distance teaching through online provision. Many studies indicate that the future belongs to dual-mode institutions which are likely to thrive in the coming decade.

The mixed-mode has evolved from the dual-mode universities, and was initiated mainly by on-campus students, that took online courses concurrently with attending regular face-to-face sessions (Ho and Burnsike, 2005; Hoffman, 2005; Hong, 2008; Howell et al., 2003; Martyn, 2003; Pittinsky, 2003; Saba, 2006). Ten years ago , it came as a surprise in some universities when some enrolled students on campus decided to take courses online in preference to attending classes on campus (American Federation of Teachers, 2001; Bradburn, 2002; Trow, 1999). Those students have testified that they are glad to have the freedom to do the work of these online courses at their own convenience and their own speed, and that they like the combination of the two types of academic delivery. Nowadays it is a most popular option and it is likely to expand considerably in the future.

'Virtual universities' constitute a most diverse group. This group contains all higher education institutions that are relying more, than any of their predecessors, on the delivery of online education (Pollock and Cornford, 2002). Some operate just as a website with little content of their own (as was the California's Virtual University that has closed a few years ago). Many are private ventures, while a few are sponsored by national governments. Some are offering a whole range of academic degrees, whereas most of the others provide a limited number of professional diplomas and continuing education courses. Many of the corporate universities, discussed earlier in Chapter 4, operate as virtual universities. Virtual universities are delivering their courses through different technologies and are based on diverse organizational infrastructures. The National Technology University in the US, for instance, operates as a mediator between leading universities (such as MIT and Berkeley) and hundreds of business enterprises. It has no academic faculty of its own. It offers a limited number of graduate level courses in engineering through teleconferencing by a satellite. A small percentage of the students who take these courses are earning credits towards degrees. The bulk is engaged in professional continuing education.

The Western Governors University that was established in 1996 constitutes an interesting model. It was set as a very ambitious enterprise between 19 Western American states as a non-profit, independent corporation with a board of trustees composed of the governors from each participating state. Its Advisory Board consists of representatives from major corporations and private foundations that provide ongoing support and advice to the university (Western Governors University, 2008). It was planned as a fully-accredited university empowered to grant degrees on demonstrated competencies that will be recognized by both employers and the academia. It is actually the only accredited university in the US that offers competency-based online degrees, and as such constitutes a novel model in academia. The emphasis on assessing competencies, whether learning has occurred, rather than on who provided the learning and how long the student attended classes, constitutes a most daring and challenging notion. So far, the Western Governors University has not realized its initial promise, and operates on a most limited scale. It offers a handful of licensure programs, bachelor programs and an MBA program.

The new technologies gave also rise to a large number of diploma mills, which Daniel Levy calls them 'Fly by Night Institutions' (Levy, 2008). Noble (2001) cautioned that 'Digital Diploma Mills' have introduced a regressive trend in the academic world, which is directed mainly towards a rather old era of mass-production, standardization and purely commercial interests. Only efficient quality control mechanisms can guard against the destructive effects of many diploma mills and false academic institutions that pride themselves by offering 'prestigious academic degrees by non-accredited institutions' as many of us receive frequently as trash e-mails.

Online education is likely to attract in the future several new adult student constituencies. Today, lifelong learning has become the leitmotif and dominant slogan of most higher education institutions worldwide. *Grosso modo*, lifelong learning is based on part-time education proceeding throughout the whole life cycle. Part-time students are typically adults in full or partial employment and/or having family and social commitments. Among the older students at least three distinct groups can be identified: second-chance students; professional workers; and adults seeking to broaden their education in order to become better acquainted with new fields of knowledge. The proportion of students joining online education for professional upgrade and for recreational purposes will grow immensely in the future.

A large proportion of students in any higher education institution will be studying towards various diplomas and continuing education courses, rather than towards full degree programs. International students, composed of young professionals working in international corporations, will be a growing component in higher education institutions offerings courses and programs fully online or through a blended model. Being highly mobile they will expect to continue studying as they move within or between different national jurisdictions.

ENHANCING FLEXIBILITY

E-learning will greatly contribute to a growing flexibility in academic study patterns (Bates, 2001, 2005; Boezerooij, 2006; Collis and Moonen, 2001; Collis and van der Wende, 200; Dickard, 2003; Duderstadt, 2000; Duderstadt et al., 2002, 2005; Mena, 2007; Scott et al., 2006; Wilson, 2001). Flexible learning offers students many opportunities to adjust their interests, needs and learning styles to a variety of learning settings and media combinations. Hybrid courses, combining various components of face-to-face encounters with online provision, simulations, participation in virtual reality scenarios, will emerge as a growing pattern in academic institutions. Dede claimed that nowadays people want increasingly educational products and services tailored to their individual needs rather than one-size-fits-all courses of fixed length, content and pedagogy. But he also attested that: "These are admittedly speculations rather than based on extensive evidence" (Dede, 2005, p. 8). Such tailored-made programs, mainly in professional update programs and at the graduate and post-graduate levels are likely to increase in the future.

Bates indicated that the fact that students and teachers no longer need to be in the same time or space for effective learning to occur "leads to greater flexibility and convenience for both learners and teachers, and probably more effective learning", even in campus-based universities (Bates, 2005, p. 147). Bates (2005) distinguished between: technology-enhanced classroom teaching; distance learning; and distributed learning. Distributed learning is a mix of a deliberately reduced face-to-face teaching and online learning. For the most part, faculty who make e-learning a part of their teaching do so by having the new technologies simplify tasks and add-on functions, not by fundamentally changing how the subject is taught.

Zemsky and Massy (2004a) indentified four areas of adoption of the digital technologies in academic environments: (1) Enhancement to traditional course/program configurations – such applications inject new materials into learning and teaching processes without changing the basic mode of instruction. Examples include e-mail communication, student access to information on the Internet, and the use of multimedia and simple simulations; (2) Course management systems - which enable professors and students to interact more effectively. They provide better communication with and among students, quick access to course materials, and support for administering and grading examinations. A special subset of these activities come bundled together to enable the creation of true online courses and learning networks; (3) Imported course objects - which enable professors to embed a richer variety of materials into their courses than is possible with traditional 'do it yourself' learning devices. Examples range from compressed video presentations to complex interactive simulations. Online entities are springing up to collect, refine, distribute, and support learning objects; (4) New course/program configurations - which result when faculty and their institutions re-engineer teaching and learning activities to take an optimal advantage of the new technology. They also require professors and students to accept new roles - with each other and with technology and support staff. These four areas of e-learning innovations are currently in different stages of their adoption cycles.

Zemsky and Massy found in their study that more than 60% of the academic faculty use e-learning mainly in terms of course enhancements.

Similar rates were recognized in using course management tools and computer-based assessments. There is widespread adoption of course management tools such as BlackBoard and WebCT. Academic faculty and corporate trainers are successfully integrating electronically delivered learning materials into literally thousands of courses focusing on both traditional and non-traditional subjects. Less usage takes place when it comes to developing comprehensive e-learning courses or using course material developed by others (Zemsky and Massy, 2004a).

Some entitle the 'distributed learning' as 'hybrid courses'. Hybrid courses emerge as a popular future trend. Hybrid courses can be designed in the framework of a specific course, which combines face-to-face encounters and online teaching, or in a program framework where most courses are taught in a conventional face-to-face setting, and some courses are taken fully or partially online. Some universities encourage the blended model by requiring their students to take at least 10% of their courses online. The Sloan Report indicated that in the US more than half (55.6%) of the higher education institutions in 2002 offered online and blended courses and a further 9.6% offered blended-only courses (Allen and Seaman, 2004). The reasons why universities provide some courses online can vary widely, from a desire to provide students with a wider choice of learning opportunities (by even taking courses from another higher education institution), to the need to alleviate pressure on teaching space.

Bates argued that blended learning provides an ideal mode of delivery particularly for lifelong learners and that in knowledge-based economies lifelong learning has become critical for economic development and extremely attractive to the private sector. Bates estimated that lifelong learning for professional and update education in the near future will be at least great as the market for students leaving high school for university and college (Bates, 2007).

Changing Roles of Academic Faculty

Academics relate differently to the employment of the advanced technologies in their research as compared to teaching. Most professors have adopted the new technologies enthusiastically in their research. All forms of research activities are influenced today by the new technologies. Data retrieval and generation, data administration and representation, as well as scientific communication and collaboration are all affected by the information and communication technologies. The introduction of e-mail and the Internet capabilities have increased enormously connectivity and interaction among scholars, located both remote from each other or situated even in the same campus, and have prompted the creation of many research networks. The US scholars have had a unique role in both harnessing the new technologies for enhancing research networks and for leading the knowledge distributed system. Most of today's influential journals which are widely read and cited are edited and published in the US.

Altbach (2005) claims that the fact that technological innovations such as the use of the Internet for scholarly communications, online journals, bibliographical services, and document delivery through computer-based means have all been developed and are most widespread in the US, explains the dominant leadership role of the American scholars in shaping the research agendas of most academic communities. Altbach remarks that: "It is perhaps significant that only American e-mail addresses do not have to list a country identifier – an artifact, no doubt, of the American origins of the Internet, and symbolic of US domination of this key communication tool" (ibid, p. 151). The primacy of the American professoriate in utilizing the digital technologies for knowledge generation and knowledge transmission turns them to be in the center of the international knowledge network. Their research agendas and publication platforms tend to be the most influential, because they are the key decision makers, as well as the major users of the new knowledge systems. American universities dominate all of the league tables of prominent research universities. Scholars at leading universities in other countries follow the suit of American research universities, and mobilize the various uses of the information and communication technologies to advance their research agendas (Chodorow, 2000; Welch, 2005).

International networks of academic researchers are replacing today national and institutional cultures of research (Douglass, 2005; Heinecke et al., 2001; Masi and Winder, 2005; National Research Council, 2002; O'Brien, 2005). We are currently experiencing a shift, from a broad campus community of faculty to international communities of scholars working on specific areas of study. The common bond of faculty teaching and working with colleagues on a campus is weakening, and as such it has changed the nature of academic research which has developed through hundreds of years. This is a natural progression. As academic fields have matured, specialization has increased and the need to interact with colleagues from different institutions has become a widely recognized phenomenon critical for the advancement of research and knowledge. Unquestionably, this shift has been facilitated greatly by the development of the Internet, which makes academic interaction with colleagues from throughout the world more practical and ubiquitous.

Unlike the research domain, many academics feel reluctant to use the digital technologies in their teaching, for reasons that were discussed broadly in Chapters 2 and 3. Academics that teach in various-type higher education institutions are required nowadays to assume new roles in order to be able to design blended or online courses. Many studies specify a long list of roles which teachers are expected to undertake when utilizing the new technologies in their teaching (Bates and Poole, 2003; Beaudoin, 2006a; Hawkins, 2006; Laurillard, 2002; Moe and Blodgett, 2000; Moore and Kearsley, 2005; National Staff Development Council, 2001; Shea et al., 2006; Stephenson, 2001; Wallace, 2004). As aforementioned they are expected to: Provide syllabi, instructional resources, communication tools, and learning strategies; monitor and assess learning and provide feedback, remediation, and grades; identify and resolve instructional, interpersonal, and technical problems; and create a learning community in which learners feel safe and connected and believe their contributions are valid (Wilson et al., 2004). Definitely a long list of responsibilities which most of the professors have not been prepared for in their socialization processes into the academic world.

It is quite clear that there exists a burning need to develop incentives in order to promote effective teacher participation in various modes of online teaching. Of particular importance is an ongoing and just-in-time support. Many institutions acknowledge the need to recruit in the future a broader range of personnel to complement academic staff, such as technologists, instructional designers, learning scientists, etc., in order to implement the technologies more effectively. Academics will have to become in the future reconciled to collaborating with other colleagues and professionals in designing materials and in the teaching process. They will need to learn how to collaborate in a team framework with tutors, editors, instructional designers, television producers, computer experts, graphic production personnel, etc. in developing and delivering their courses.

The new technologies will require the academic faculty to assume new responsibilities and to develop a range of new skills. At the same time, teachers will have greater flexibility to choose the teaching styles which are better suited for their personal strengths and individual preferences. Universities will have to deliberate how to prepare the new generations of academic faculty to operate in a world where blended courses and online teaching are an integral part of the academic teaching responsibilities.

CONSOLIDATING RESEARCH FINDINGS ON TEACHING AND LEARNING

There is a common agreement in many studies that time has come to consolidate the multiple research findings on the use of the digital technologies for various purposes in academic environments into coherent findings that will assist to illuminate the most important conclusions as to what really affects successful teaching and efficient learning. Martin Trow claimed in 1999 that there is an urgent need of comprehensive research on the technologies' applications: "We need research in this area because while we can say with some confidence that the new forms of instruction will have large effects, for most part we do not know the nature of those effects, nor their costs, material or human" (Trow, 1999, p. 203). This urgent need to investigate the multiple effects of the new technologies on higher education and harmonize them into a comprehensive framework is still existent, but there are some inherent difficulties in conducting research on the applications of the new technologies. One inherent limitation of the current and future research on the new technologies is tied to their speed of development. The development of the new electronic media is very fast. As such it poses difficulties for researchers who find it difficult to conduct longitudinal studies on the digital media's effects and capabilities. Research in academia is characterized by the ability of the researchers to examine any investigated phenomenon from a perspective of time and through a relatively long reflective process of deliberation and trials. The speed of the electronic technologies' development inhibits this very basic characteristic of academic research. Researchers do not possess the luxury to examine the influences of the new technologies on human learning from a distant perspective and over time, since the entities they are starting to investigate might become obsolete at the time their conclusions are drawn. It follows, that the academics' tendency to examine new phenomena rationally and carefully is strongly reduced by the uncertainties of the future technological developments.

An excellent example as to the inherent difficulty to project definite future impacts of the information and communication technologies on higher education is provided by a wide-range study launched by the National Academies of the USA to investigate the impact of the new technologies on the future of the research universities (National Research Council, 2002). At the conclusion section, the honorable panel members of this study apologize for not being able to provide definite recommendations as how to proceed with the implementation of the technologies in research universities: "Although part of its charge was to make policy recommendations, the panel ultimately decided not to do so in this first phase of activity. One factor in this decision was that information technology is evolving so rapidly that any perspective set of conclusions and recommendations could quickly become outdated. Also, the panel was unable to examine the numerous issues bearing on the topic… with the depth needed for recommending policy changes" (ibid, p. 49).

Many studies, on the implementation of the digital technologies in higher education, stress that time has come to design a robust data collection strategy in order to develop a catalogue of lessons learned, both from past successes as well as from failures. Mackintosh (2006) suggested complementing such an analysis of lessons learned from past experience with conceptual modeling techniques with a future focus by alternative future scenarios. It is important for e-learning designers to resolve questions regarding what students expect from e-learning.

Duderstadt et al. (2002) argued that higher education must, like other organizations, identify its real strengths, and 'unbundle' those activities in which the digital technologies do not have a unique advantage or ability. Successful organizations are able to capitalize on sustaining technologies and avoid disruptive ones, but colleges and universities typically react more slowly, and so remain more vulnerable.

Gradual Change of Academic Environments

Digital technologies have penetrated higher education in various domains. They have affected educational governance and administration; academic publishing practices; library management; strengthening of research communities; mobility of students and faculty between institutions; enhanced communication with instructors in- and after classes; growing communication amongst students; new ways of presenting various subject matters, etc. Such changes have affected eventually the academic culture and the shape of higher education environments, and are likely to have even deeper effects in the future. In the conclusions of the comprehensive OECD study which was conducted in higher education institutions in 13 different countries, it was emphasized that: "The limited impact of IT in the classroom seen to date should not be dismissed as a lack of innovation or change in tertiary education as a whole: even if IT does not induce any change in the classroom, it is changing the learning experience of students by relaxing time and space constraints as well as providing easier access to information (online journals and e-books, student portals, etc,) and greater flexibility of participation" (OECD, 2005, p. 15). In other words, even if the new technologies have not transformed dramatically the traditional face-to-face encounters, the changes in the surrounding environment have an impact on the essence of the teaching/learning practices. As already discussed in Chapter 2, it seems that the future transformation of academe will continue to be evolutionary rather than revolutionary, but still most meaningful in the long run.

The reorganization of libraries constitutes one of the most dramatic changes in academic environments which affects greatly the work of researchers, teachers and students. The Internet has made easily available a plethora of books, magazines, and journals that turned the old organization of the brick and mortar libraries of the traditional universities non effective and forced them to restructure their operation (Winston, 2006). However, students need now more then ever to be taught how to filter and use all of the information available to them at such ease.

Bates claimed that the main reason for the piecemeal adoption of the digital technologies is the fact that most higher education institutions still operate on the underlying logic of an industrial society: "The industrial revolution, with its need to educate large numbers of people for commercial life, led to mass education, and the large group method of teaching was the most economical way to provide this. However, while in the twentieth-century technology has revolutionized communications, leading to the information society, our educational institutions are still pickled in the aspic of the industrial revolution" (Bates, 2005, p. 225). Some researchers agree that the need to redesign teaching and learning, and to reorganize institutions to support the use of technology in both teaching and administration, is the greatest challenge facing higher education today.

EMERGENCE OF NEW TECHNOLOGIES

We had briefly mentioned in Chapter 4 the emerging mobile technologies. It is quite clear that at the present time, the models for the use and development of mobile applications for learning are somewhat limited. However, it is obvious that the whole world is becoming today mobile. Phones, computers and media devices now fit in our pockets and can connect us to a variety of information sources and enable communication nearly everywhere we go (Hill and Roldan, 2005; Naismith et al., 2005). Today we are witnessing the emergence of a connected, mobile society, with a variety of information resources and means of communication at home, work, school and in the community at large. According to Attewell (2005) there were approximately 1.5 billion mobile phones in 2003, and it is most likely that this figure has doubled since then (Motlik, 2008).

The current trends in mobile computing are towards devices that are even more embedded, ubiquitous and networked than those available today. The capabilities of mobile phones, game consoles, and cameras will likely merge within the next five to ten years to provide a networked, multimedia device that can accompany everyone, anytime, anywhere. The entire Internet will become both personal and portable. Such technologies hold great promise, most particularly for developing countries.

There are already a few pilot studies related to the application of mobile technologies in certain areas. Thornton and Houser (2004) studied the use of mobile phones in Japan to teach English as a second language. Mobile phones in Japan outnumbered in 2003 PCs in a proportion of five to one. Student scores among mobile phone users were the same as those for traditional test takers. Thornton and Houser concluded in their study that 71% of the students liked receiving lessons on their mobile phones better than on PCs, 93% found mobile phones to be valuable for teaching; and 89% wanted to continue using their mobiles for educational purposes. Ramos, Tritona and Lambert (2006) reported that educational uses of mobile phones have increased dramatically in the Philippines. The Open University of the Philippines already has formal

SMS-based mobile courses in English, math, and sciences. 80% of the students surveyed in this study embraced the idea of learning through SMS. The educational use of mobile phones is also gaining momentum in Africa. Visser and West (2005) indicated that in South Africa less than 11% of the population owns a landline telephone as compared to 90% of the country's population that have access to cellular phones. Visser and West noted that the next generation of mobile phones "have started to include full Internet access and introduce an always-on cellular technology which enables the cellular telephone user to access the Internet directly" (ibid, p. 120). The advent of cheaper handsets and better services will accelerate the rate of users of mobile technologies. However, it is too early to estimate the potential effects of the mobile technologies. Like in most of the studies on digital technologies, the first generation of adopters tends always to be enthusiastic about the opportunities and possibilities of new technology which they like and are eager to promote.

The immersive technologies constitute a totally different type of new emerging technologies (Ferdig, 2008; Immersive Education, 2008; Lamont, 2008). These technologies are currently employed by over hundred universities and colleges in the US and are also gaining momentum in other parts of the world. They are complex and expensive and fit currently mainly the wealthy and well-to-do higher education institutions.

The Immersive Education Initiative is an international collaboration of universities, colleges, research institutes, consortia and companies that work together to define and develop platforms, best practices, for virtual reality and game-based learning and training systems. Immersive Education combines interactive 3D graphics, commercial game and simulation technology, virtual reality, voice chat, Web cameras and rich digital media. "Immersive Education gives participants a sense of 'being there' even when attending a class or training session in person isn't possible, practical, or desirable, which in turn provides educators and students with the ability to connect and communicate in a way that greatly enhances the learning experience" (Immersive Education, 2008).

Originally, the Immersive Education Platform was available only to students that belonged to well-established higher education institutions, like the Harvard University Extension. The next generation of Immersive Education is focused on a broad spectrum of academic and non-academic users in higher education, corporate training and K-12 (kindergarten through high school). Obviously, the platform of Immersive Education is rich and expensive: "It is designed to immerse and engage students in the same way that today's best video games grab and keep the attention of the players" (ibid). It has a great potential to be attractive to both students and teachers. At the same time it has also the potential to widen the digital gap between rich and poor, developed and developing countries. There is already an initiative led by Boston College in cooperation with the Grid Institute, Burke Institute for Innovation in Education, Media Machines, City of Boston, Sun Microsystems and some other organizations to make Immersive Education available as a community resource for the benefit of educators, students and researchers – an example of a philanthropic open source initiative, that at this stage will benefit mainly well-established higher education institutions. Only in a retrospect of ten to twenty years it will be possible to examine the effects of these new and rich technologies on higher education environments.

REFERENCES

Aadelsberger, H., Collis, B. and Pawlowski, J. (Eds.) (2002). *Handbook of Information Technologies for Education and Training.* Berlin: Springer Verlag.

Abel, R. (2005). Implementing the Best Practices in Online Learning, *EDUCAUSE Quarterly, 28* (3), 75-77.

Adkins, S. S. (2002). *Market Analysis of the 2002 US E-learning Industry: Convergence, Consolidation, and Commoditization.* Sunnyvale, CA.: Brandon-Hall.

Adelman, C. (2000). *A Parallel Universe Expanded: Certification in the Information Technology Guild.* http://aahe.org/change/paralleluniverse.htm

Ali, A. and Elfessi, A. (2004). Examining Students' Performance and Attitudes towards the Use of Information Technology in a Virtual and Conventional Setting, *Journal of Interactive Online Learning, 2* (3), 1-9.

Allen, E. and Seaman, J. (2003). *Seizing the Opportunity: The Quality and Extent of Online Education in the United States, 2002 and 2003.* Needham and Wellesley, MA: The Sloan Consortium, A Consortium of Institutions and Organizations Committed to Quality Online Education.

Allen, E. and Seaman, J. (2004). *Entering the Main Stream: The Quality and Extent of Online Education in The United States, 2003 and 2004.* Needham and Wellesley, MA: The Sloan Consortium, A Consortium of Institutions and Organizations Committed to Quality Online Education.

Altbach, P. (2004). Globalization and the University: Myths and Realities in an Unequal World, *Tertiary Education and Management, 1,* 63-73.

Altbach, P. (2005). Academic Challenges: The American Professoriate in Comparative Perspective. In: A. Welch (Ed.), *The Professoriate: Profile of a Profession.* Dordrecht: Springer, 147-165.

Altbach, P. and Balan, J. (Eds.) (2007). *World Class Worldwide: Transforming Research Universities in Asia and Latin America.* Baltimore: The Johns Hopkins University Press.

American Association of University Women (2001). *The Third Shift: Women Learning Online.* Washington, D. C.

American Federation of Teachers (2000). *Distance Education: Guidelines for Good Practice.* Washington D.C.

American Federation of Teachers (2001). *A Virtual Revolution: Trends in the Expansion of Distance Education.* Washington D.C.

Anderson, T. and Elloumi, F. (2004). *Theory and Practice of Online Learning.* Athabasca University, Canada.

Anglin, G. and Morrison, G. (2000). An Analysis of Distance Education Research: Implications for the Instructional Technologist, *Quarterly Review of Distance Education, 1* (3), 189-194.

Arafeh, S. (2004). *The Implications of Information and Communications Technologies for Distance Education: Looking Toward the Future.* Arlington, VA: SRI International, Final Report, P11913.

Arnold, R. (1999). Will Distance Disappear in Distance Studies? Preliminary Considerations on the Didactic Relevance of Proximity and Distance, *Journal of Distance Education, 14* (2), 1-9.

Ashby, C. (2002). *Growth in Distance Education Programs and Implications for Federal Education Policy (GAO-02-1125T).* Washington, D.C.: US General Accounting Office.

Attewell, J. (2005). *Mobile Technologies and Learning: A Technology Update and M-Learning Project Summary.* London: Learning and Skills Development Agency.

Aycock, A., Garnham, C. and Kaleta, R. (2002). Lessons Retrieved from the Hybrid Course Project, *Teaching with Technology Today, 8* (6).

Ayers, E. (2005). Harmonizing the Realm of Academe and IT, *Education Review,* November-December.

Baggaley, B. and Belawati, T. (Eds.) (2007). *Distance Education Technology in Asia.* Lahore: Virtual University of Pakistan.

Barajas, M. (2003). *Monitoring and Evaluation of Research in Learning Innovations-MERLIN.* Brussels: Unit of Research in the Social Sciences and Humanities, European Commission.

Barnett, R. (2000). *Realizing the University in an Age of Supercomplexity.* Buckingham: The Society of Research into Higher Education and Open University Press.

Barrow, C. W., Didou-Aupetit, S. and Mallea, J. (2003). *Gloablisation, Trade Liberalisation, and Higher Education in North America.* Dordrecht: Kluwer Academic Publishers.

Bartels, J. and Peters, O. (1986). The German Fernuniversität; Its Main Features and Function. In: G. Van Enckevort, K. Harry and H. G. Schutze (Eds.), *Distance Education and the Adult Learner.* Herleen: Dutch Open University, 97-110.

Bates, A. W. (1999). *Managing Technological Change: Strategies for Academic Leaders*. San-Francisco: Jossey Bass.

Bates, A. W. (2001). *National Strategies for E-learning in Post-Secondary Education and Training.* Paris: International Institute for Educational Planning, UNESCO.

Bates, A.W. (2005). *Technology, E-Learning and Distance Education.* London: Routledgefalmer, 2nd Edition.

Bates, A. W. (2007). *Distance Education in a Knowledge-Based Society,* A Keynote Address in the ICDE Conference on 'The Metamorphosis of Distance Education in the Third Millennium', Toluca, Mexico.

Bates, A. W. and Poole, G. (2003). *Effective Teaching with Technology in Higher Education: Foundations for Success.* San-Francisco: Jossey-Bass.

Bauder, H. (2006). The Segmentation of Academic Labour: A Canadian Example, *ACME Journal, 4,* 228-239.

Beaudoin, M. F. (Ed.) (2006a). *Perspectives on Higher Education in the Digital Age.* New York: Nova Science.

Beaudoin, M. F. (2006b). The Impact of Distance Education on the Academy in the Digital Age. In: M. F. Beaudoin (Ed.) (2006). *Perspectives on Higher Education in the Digital Age.* New York: Nova Science, 1-20.

Bell, R. and Tight, M. (1993). *Open Universities: A British Tradition.* Buckingham: The Society of Research into Higher Education and the Open University Press.

Bernard, R. M., Abrami, P. C., Lou, Y., Borokhovski, E. and Al, E. (2004). How Does Distance Education Compare with Classroom Instruction: A

Meta-Analysis of the Empirical Literature, *Review of Educational Research, 74* (3), 345-379.

Bernath, U. and Hulsmann, T. (2004). Low Cost/High Outcome Approaches in Open, Distance and E-learning. In: U. Bernath and A. Szcus (Eds.) *Supporting the Learner in Distance Education and E-learning: Proceedings of the Third EDEN Research Workshop.* Oldenburg: Bibliotheks-Und-Informationssytem Der Universitat Oldenburg, 485-491.

Bitzer, J. and Schroder, P. (Eds.) (2006). *The Economics of Open Source Software Development.* Elsevier.

Blumenstyk, G. (2001). Temple University Shuts Down For-Profit Distance Education Company, *Chronicle of Higher Education,* 20 July.

Blumenstyk, G. (2003). For-Profit Colleges Attract a Gold Rush for Investors, *The Chronicle of Higher Education*, 14 March.

Boezerooij, P. (2006). *E-Learning Strategies of Higher Education Institutions.* Enschede: CHEPS.

Boezerooy, P., Collis, B. and Van Der Wende (2002). *Models of Technology and Change in Higher Education: An International Comparative Survey on the Current and Future Uses of ICT in Higher Education,* Paper presented at 24th Annual EAIR Forum, Prague, September.

Bok, D. (2004). *Universities in the Market Place.* Princeton University Press.

Borek, B. (2005). VW Partners With Stanford Focus on Industrial Design, *The Stanford Daily,* May 12.

Boume, J., Mayadas, F. and Moore, J. (2005). *Review of the Report on: 'Thwarted Innovation: What Happened To E-learning And Why'.* The Sloan Consortium, A Consortium of Institutions and Organizations Committed to Quality Online Education.

Bradburn, E. M. (2002). *Distance Education Instruction by Postsecondary Faculty and Staff at Degree-Granting Institutions,* Washington, D.C.: U.S. Department of Education, National Center for Education Statistics, NCES 2002-155.

Bridges Organization (2003). *Spanning the Digital Divide: Understanding and Tackling the Issues.* http://www.bridges.org/spanning_the_digital_divide.pdf

Brindley, J. E., Walti, C. and Zawacki-Richter, O. (Eds.) (2004). *Learner Support in Open, Distance and Online Learning Environments.* Oldenburg: Bibliotheks-Und Informationssystem Der Universität Oldenburg.

Bullen, M. (2005). *Preserving The Social Mandate of Distance Education,* Invited Presentation to the Congreso Internacional *UFF/CREAD,* Niteroi, Brazil.

Bullen, M. and Janes, D. (Eds.) (2006). *Making The Transition To E-Learning: Issues And Strategies.* Hershey, PA: The Idea Group.

Caelis International (2004). *The Future Role of Information and Communication Technologies in Education and Training in Asia and The Pacific.* Prepared for the Development Bank. Vancouver: Publisher.

Candy, P. C. (2004). *Linking, Thinking: Self-Directed Learning in the Digital Age.* Department of Education, Science and Training, Commonwealth of Australia.

Carlson, S. (2002). *The Missing Link in Educational Technology: Trained Teachers.* http://www.technowlogia.org/tkl_active_pages2/cyrrentarticles/main.asp?issuenumber=18andfiletype=pdfandarticleid=435

Carlson, S. (2003a). Old Computers Never Die - They Just Cost Colleges Money in New Ways, *The Chronicle of Higher Education,* 14 February.

Carlson, S. (2003b). After Losing Millions, Columbia University will Close its Online-Learning Venture, *The Chronicle of Higher Education,* 7 January.

Carmichael, P. and Honour, L. (2002). *Open Source as Appropriate Technology for Global Education.* http://www.col.org/tel199/acrobat/carmichael.pdf

Carneavale, D. (2004). Report Says Educational Technology Has Failed to Deliver its Promises, *The Chronicle of Higher Education, 50* (43), A30.

Carr, S. (2000). Psych Students Learn More Through Distance Ed but Are Less Satisfied, *Chronicle of Higher Education,* February 14, 21,A48.

Castells, M. (2000). *The Rise of the Network Society.* Oxford, England: Blackwell Publishers.

CHEPS (2002). Successful Conference on ICT in Rotterdam, *CHEPS Unplugged,* 2 (3), 2.

Chickering, A. W. and Ehrmann, S. C. (1996). Implementing the Seven Principles: Technology as Lever, *AAHE Bulletin, 49* (2), 3-6

Chickering, A. W. and Gamson, Z. F. (1987). Seven Principles for Good Practice in Undergraduate Education, *AAHE Bulletin 39* (7), 3-7.

Chickering, A. W. and Gamson, Z. F. (1991). Applying the Seven Principles for Good Practice in Undergraduate Education, *New Directions in Teaching and Learning.* San Francisco: Jossey-Bass.

Chodorow, S. (2000). Scholarship and Scholarly Communication in The Digital Age, *EDUCAUSE Review*, *35*, January/February, 86-92.

Clancy, P., Eggins, H., Goastellec, G., Guri-Rosenblit, S, Nguyen, P. N and Yizengaw, T. (2007). Comparative Aspects on Access and Equity. In: P. Altbach and Peterson, P. M. (Eds.). *Higher Education in the New Century: Global Challenges and Innovative Ideas.* Rotterdam: Sense Publishers, 35-54.

Clark, B. R. (1986). Implementation in the US: A Comparison with European Higher Education. In: L Cerych and P. Sabatier (Eds.), *Great Expectations and Mixed Performances: The Implementation of Higher Education Reforms in Europe,* European Institute of Educational and Social Policy. Stoke-on-Trent: Trentham Books.

Clark, B. R. (1998). *Creating Entrepreneurial Universities: Organizational Pathways of Transformation,* Oxford: Pergamon Press and International Association of Universities.

Clark, T. (2001). *Virtual Schools: Trends and Issues: A Study of Virtual Schools in the United States.* San Francisco: Distance Learning Network, Wested.

Clarke, A. (1999). 2001 – A Cyber Odyssey: Arthur Clarke's Optimistic Guide to Surviving the Information Age, *Himalmag, 12* (11), November.

Cohen, D. (2005). Speakers Give Contrasting Views of Academic Caliber of Australia's Foreign Student Market, *The Chronicle of Higher Education*, October 17th.

Collis, B. (1995). Networking and Distance Learning for Telematics: A Classification of Possibilities, *Journal of Information Technology for Teacher Education*, *4* (2), 117-135.

Collis, B. and Moonen, J. (2001). *Flexible Learning in a Digital World: Experience and Expectations*. London: Kogan Page.

Collis, B. and Van Der Wende, M. (2002). Models of Change: ICT and the Internationalization of Higher Education, *Journal of Studies in International Education, 6* (2), 87-100.

Cooper, J. and Weaver, K. D. (2003). *Gender and Computers: Understanding the Digital Divide.* Mahwah, NJ: Lawrence Erlbaum Associates.

Cox, M. and Marshall, G. (2007). Effects of ICT: Do We Know What We Should Know?, *Education and Information Technologies, 12* (2), 59-70.

Cox, M., Webb, M., Abbott, C., Blakeley, B., Beauchamp, T and Rhodes, V. (2004). *ICT in Pedagogy: A Review of the Research Literature.* London: British Educational Communications and Technology Agency.

Cross, P. K. (2005). *What Do We Know About Students' Learning and how Do We Know it?* Research and Occasional Papers Series, CSHE 7.05, UC Berkeley.

Cuban, L. (2001). *Oversold and Underused: Computers in the Classroom.* Cambridge: Harvard University Press.

Cummings, J. A., Bonk, C. J. and Jacobs, F. R. (2002). Twenty-First Century College Syllabi: Options for Online Communication and Interaction, *The Internet and Higher Education, 5* (1), 1-19.

Curran, C. (2001). The Phenomenon of On-Line Learning, *European Journal of Education, 36*(2), 113-132.

Curran, C. (2004). *Strategies for E-Learning in Universities.* Research and Occasional Papers Series, CSHE 7.04, UC Berkeley.

Currie, J. (2005). Globalisation's Impact on the Professioriate in Anglo-American Universities. In: A. Welch (Ed.). *The Professoriate: Profile of a Profession.* Dordrecht: Springer, 21-34.

Currie, J., Deangelis, R., De Boar, H., Huisman, J. and Lacotte, C. (2003). *Globalization Practices and University Responses: European and Anglo-American Differences.* Westport, Ct: Greenwood Publishers.

Daniel, J. S. (1990). Distance Education in Developing Countries. In: M. Croft, I. Mugridge, J. S. Daniel and A. Hershfield (Eds.), *Distance Education: Development and Access.* Caracas: ICDE Proceedings, 101-102.

Daniel, J. S. (1996). *The Mega-Universities and the Knowledge Media*, London: Kogan Page.

De Ferranti, D. and Perry, G. E. (2003). *Closing the Gap in Education and Technology.* Washington, D.C.: The World Bank.

Dede, C. (1995). The Transformation of Distance Education to Distributed Learning, *Instructional Technology Research Online.*

Dede, C. (2005). Planning for Neo-Millennial Learning Styles, *Educause Quarterly, 28* (1), 7-12.

Derntl, M. and Motsching-Pitrik, R. (2005). The Role of Structure, Patterns and People in Blended Learning, *Internet and Higher Education, 8* (2), 111-130.

Dickard, N. (2003). *The Sustainability Challenge: Taking Edtech to the Next Level.* Washington D.C.: Benton Foundation.

Disessa, A. (2000). *Changing Minds: Computers, Learning and Literacy.* Cambridge, MA: MIT Press.

Dogramaci, A. (2008). Private University Initiatives in Turkey: The Bilkent University, Paper presented at the Conference on 'Privatization in Higher Education', Haifa: Samuel Neeman Institute, The Technion.

Donnelly, R. and Mcsweeney, F. (Eds.) (2008). *Applied E-Learning and E-Teaching in Higher Education.* Hershey: Information Science Reference.

Donohue, B. and Howe-Steiger, L. (2005). Faculty and Administrators Collaborating for E-Learning Courseware, *Educause Quarterly, 28* (1), 20-32.

Douglass, J. A. (2001). A Reflection and Prospects on California Higher Education: The Beginning of a New History, *California Policy Issues,* November 2001, 81-156.

Douglass, J. A. (2005). *All Globalization is Local: Countervailing Forces and the Influence on Higher Education Markets.* UC Berkeley: Research and Occasional Paper Series, 1.05.

Dowd, R. J. (2006). *Copyright Litigation Handbook.* Thomson West.

Drucker, P. F. (1997) Seeing Things as They Really Are. *Forbes,* March 10th, 1997.

Drucker, P. F. (1998). The Future has already Happened, *Futurist, 32* (8), 16-19.

Duderstadt, J. (2000). *A University for The 21st Century.* Ann Arbor: University Michigan Press.

Duderstadt, J., Atkins, D. and Van Houweling, D. (2002). *Higher Education in the Digital Age.* Wesport, CT: Praeger.

Duderstadt, J., Wulf, W. A. and Zemsky, R. (2005). Envisioning a Transformed University, *Issues in Science and Technology, 22* (1).

Duffy, T. M. and Kirkley, J. R. (2004). *Learner-Centered Theory and Practice in Distance Education: Cases from Higher Education.* Mahwah, N.J.: L. Erlbaum.

Dunlap, J. C. (2005). Workload Reduction in Online Courses: Getting Some Shuteye, *Performance Improvement, 44* (5), 18-26.

Dupin-Bryant, P. A. (2006). Pervasive Computing: The Future of Computers in Higher Education. In: Beaudoin, M. (Ed.), *Perspectives on Higher Education in the Digital Age,* New York: Nova Science, 35-47.

Eckel, P. and King, J. (2004). *An Overview of Higher Education in the United States: Diversity, Access and the Role of the Marketplace,* American Council on Education.

Economist (2005a). *A World of Opportunity: Developing Countries See the Point of Higher Education,* September 8th.

Economist (2005b). *The Brain Business,* September 8th.

Economist (2005c). *Wandering Scholars: For Students Higher Education is Becoming a Borderless World,* September 8th.

Economist (2005d). *The Best is yet to Come: A More Market-Oriented System of Higher Education Can Do Much Better than the State-Dominated Model,* September 8th.

Economist (2005e). *Heads in the Clouds: Europe Hopes to Become the World's Pre-Eminent Knowledge-Based Economy- Not Likely,* September 8th.

Economist (2005f). *How Europe Fails its Young: The State of Europe's Higher Education is a Long-Term Threat to its Competitiveness* , September 8th.

Economist (2005g). *Secrets of Success: America's System of Higher Education is the Best in the World,* September 8th.

Economist (2005h). *Higher Ed Inc: Universities have Become much more Businesslike: But they Are still Doing the Same Thing,* September 8th.

EDUCAUSE Center for Applied Research (2006). *ECAR Study of Students and Information Technology, 2005: Convenience, Connection, Control And Learning.*
http://www.educause.edu/ers0506

Eggins, H. (2006). *Access and Equity in Higher Education: The British Case-Study,* Internal Paper, Fulbright New Century Scholars Program.

Ehrmann, S. C. (2002). *New Ideas and Additional Reading*, TLT (Teaching, Learning And Technology) Group.

Enders, J. and Fulton, O. (Eds.) (2002). *Higher Education in a Globalising World: International Trends and Mutual Observations,* Dordrecht: Kluwer Academic Publishers.

Enders, J. and Jongbloed, B. (Eds.) (2007). *Public-Private Dynamics in Higher Education: Expectations, Developments and Outcomes.* London: Transaction Publishers.

ETS (2008). Iskills Overview.
http://www.ets.org

European Commission (2004). *The Ingredients for Building a World Class University*. Brussels: Cordis RTD News, 23 April.

Evans, T. and Nation, D. (Eds.) (2000). *Changing University Teaching: Reflections on Creating Educational Technologies*. London: Kogan Page.

Farrell, G. and Wachholz, C. (Eds.) (2003). *Meta-Survey on the Use of Technologies in Education in Asia and the Pacific (2003-2004),* Bangkok: UNESCO.

Ferdig, R. E. (Ed.) (2008). *Handbook of Research on Electronic Gaming in Education.* Hershey: Information Science Reference.

Fetterman, D. M. (1998). Webs of Meaning: Computer and Internet Resources for Educational Research and Instruction*, Educational Researcher, 27* (3), 22-31.

Fink, C. And Keneny, C. J. (2003). *W(H)Ither The Digital Divide?* http://topics.developmentgateway.org/ict/rc/filedownload.do?itemid-307615

Fouche, I. (2006). A Multi-Island Situation without the Ocean: Tutors' Perceptions about Working in Isolation from Colleagues, *International Review of Research in Open and Distance Learning, 7* (2).

Gallagher, S. (2004). *Online Distance Education Market Update: A Nascent Market Begins to Mature.* Boston, MA: Eduventures, Inc.

Gallagher, S. and Newman, A. (2002). *Distance Learning at the Tipping Point: Critical Success Factors to Growing Fully Online Distance Learning Programs.* Boston: Eduventures Inc.

Gantz, J. And Rochester, J. (2005). *Pirates of The Digital Millennium.* Prentice Hall.

Garret, R. (2004a). Foreign Higher Education Activity in China. *International Higher Education.*

Garret, R. (2004b). The Real Story Behind the Failure of the UK Euniversity, *EDUCAUSE Quarterly, 27* (4).

Garret, R. and Jokivirta, L. (2004). *Online Learning in Commonwealth Universities: Selected Data from the 2004 Observatory Survey, Part 1.* Observatory on Borderless Higher Education.

Garret, R. and Verbik, L. (2004). *Online Learning in Commonwealth Universities: Selected Data from the 2004 Observatory Survey, Part 2.* Observatory on Borderless Higher Education.

Garrison, D. R. (1993). Quality Access in Distance Education: Theoretical Considerations. In: D. Keegan (Ed.), *Theoretical Principles of Distance Education.* London: Routledge, 9-21.

Garrison, D. R. (1999). Will Distance Education Disappear in Distance Studies? – A Reaction, *Journal of Distance Education, 14* (2), 1-9.

Garrison, D. R. and Anderson, T. (Eds.) (2000). *Changing University Teaching: Reflections on Creating Educational Technologies.* London: Kogan Page.

George, M. A. (2005). Internet Dominates Campus Life: Lots of Computer Time, Little of It for Academics, *Detroit Free Press,* 15 April.

Gibbons, M. (2003). Globalization and the Future of Higher Education. In: Breton, G. and Lambert, M. (Eds.). *Universities and Globalization: Private Linkages, Public Trust.* UNESCO,107-116.

Gigling, M. (2004). *Needs Assessment of ICT in Education Policy Makers in Asia and the Pacific: Towards the Development of a Toolkit for Policy Makers.* Bangkok: UNESCO.

Giordan, M. (2004). Tutoring through the Internet: How Students and Teachers Interact to Construct Meaning, *International Journal of Science Education, 26* (15), 1875-1894.

Gladieux, L. E. and Swail, W. S. (1999). *The Virtual University and Educational Opportunity: Issues of Equity and Access for the Next Generation*, Washington, D.C.: The College Board.

Gourley, B. (2008). *Higher Education Challenges in the 21st Century,* An invited lecture at the Open University of Israel, Rannana, May 21st.

Graham, C., Cagiltary, K., Lim, B., Craner, J. and Duffy, T. M. (2001). Seven Principles of Effective Teaching: A Practical Lens for Evaluating Online Courses, *The Technology Source.*

Green, K. (2001). *The National Survey of Information Technology in US Higher Education,* Campus Computing Network..

Green, M. F. (2004). GATS Update. *International Higher Education, 37*, 3-5.

Gross, E. F. (2004). Adolescent Internet Use: What We Expect, What Teens Report, *Journal of Applied Developmental Psychology, 25* (6), 633-649.

Grossman, W. (1997). Microsoft Buy into Cambridge R and D Lab, *Wired, 6.*

Guri-Rosenblit, S. (1999a). *Distance and Campus Universities: Tensions and Interactions - A Comparative Study of Five Countries.* Oxford: Pergamon Press and International Association of Universities.

Guri-Rosenblit, S. (1999b). *Differential Impacts of Information Technologies on Three Academic Environments: The Elite Sector, Mass-Oriented Universities, and Distance Teaching Institutions*, A keynote address at the 'Euro-Med Conference on Tele-Technology in Learning Environments', Tel-Aviv, October 12th.

Guri-Rosenblit, S. (1999c). The Agendas of Distance Teaching Universities: Moving from the Margins to the Center Stage of Higher Education, *Higher Education, 37*, 281-293.

Guri-Rosenblit, S. (2001a). The Tower of Babel Syndrome in the Discourse of Information Technologies in Higher Education, *Global E-Journal of Open, Flexible and Distance Education, 1* (1), 28-38.

Guri-Rosenblit, S. (2001b). Virtual Universities: Current Models and Future Trends, *Higher Education in Europe* , XXVI (4), 487-499.

Guri-Rosenblit, S. (2002). A Top Down Strategy to Enhance Information Technologies into Israeli Higher Education, *International Review of Research in Open and Distance Learning, 2* (2).

Guri-Rosenblit, S. (2004). Distance Education Teachers in the Digital Age: New Roles and Contradictory Demands. In: U. Bernath and A. Szcus (Eds.) *Supporting the Learner in Distance Education and E-Learning: Proceedings of The Third EDEN Research Workshop.* Oldenburg: Bibliotheks-Und-Informationssytem Der Universitat Oldenburg, 492-497.

Guri-Rosenblit, S. (2005a). 'Distance Education' and 'E-Learning': Not the Same Thing, *Higher Education, 49,* 467-493.

Guri-Rosenblit, S. (2005b). Eight Paradoxes in the Implementation Process of E-Learning in Higher Education, *Higher Education Policy, 18,* 5-29.

Guri-Roenblit, S. (2006). *Access and Equity in Higher Education: Historical and Cultural Context,* Internal Paper, Fulbright New Century Scholars Program.

Guri-Rosenblit, S. (2007). Higher Education in the 21st Century: Seven Pairs of Contrasting Trends. In: Enders, J. and Van Vught F. (Eds.), *Towards a Cartography of Higher Education Policy Change.* University of Twente: Center of Higher Education Policy Studies, 307-314.

Guri-Rosenblit, S., Sebkova, H. and Teichler, U. (2007). Massification and Diversity of Higher Education Systems: Interplay of Complex Dimensions, *Higher Education Policy, 20*, 373-389.

Guterman, E., Sagi, R. and Brickner, R. (2008). *Patterns of Using Technological Applications by Course-Coordinators at the Open*

University, Paper presented at a Symposium on Attitudes of Academic Faculty towards the Implementation of Technologies in Teaching, Raanana: Open University of Israel, 31 March.

Hamilton, J. (2003). Are Main Lines and Mobile Phones Substitutes or Complements? Evidence from Africa, *Telecommunications Policy, 27* (1), 109-133.

Hanna, D. (2003). Organizational Models in Higher Education: Past and Future. In: M. Moore and W. Anderson (Eds.). *Handbook of Distance Education.* New Jersey: Lawrence Erlbaum and Associates.

Hara, N. and Kling, R. (2001). Student Distress in Web-Based Distance Education, *EDUCAUSE Quarterly, 3,* 68-69.

Harasim, L. (2000). Shift Happens: Online Education asaA New Paradigm in Learning, *Internet and Higher Education, 3* (1-2), 41-61.

Harasim, L., Hiltz, S. R., Teles, L. and Turrof, M. (1995). *Learning Networks: A Field Guide to Teaching and Learning Online.* Cambridge, MA: MIT Press.

Hargittai, W. (2002). Second-Level Digital Divide: Differences in People's Online Skills. *First Monday, 7* (4).

Harley, D., Henke, J., Lawrence, S., Maher. M., Gawlik M. and Muller, P. (2002). *An Analysis of Technology Enhancement in a Large Lecture Course at UC Berkeley: Costs, Cultures, and Complexity - A Final Report.* UC Berkeley : Center for Studies in Higher Education.

Harley, D. (2002). Investing in Educational Technologies: The Challenge of Reconciling Instructional Strategies, Faculty Goals, and Student Expectations, *Journal of Studies in International Education.*

Harper, B., Hedberg, J., Bennet, S.and Lockyer, L. (2000). *Review of Research: The Online Experience.* Kensigton Park, Australia: The Australian National Training Authority.

Hartman,. J., Dziuban, C. and Moskal, P. (2005). Preparing the Academy of Today for the Learner of Tomorrow. In: D. G. Oblinger and J. L. Oblinger (Eds.), *Educating the Next Generation.* Boulder, Co: EDUCAUSE.

Hawkins, R. (2002). *Ten Lessons for ICT and Education in the Developing World.* Boston: Harvard Center for International Development.

Hawkins, B. L. (2006). Twelve Habits of Successful IT Professionals, *EDUCAUSE Review, 41* (1), 56-67.

Heafner, T. (2004). Using Technology to Motivate Students to Learn Social Studies, *Contemporary Issue in Technology and Teacher Education, 41*(1).

Heinecke, W., Dawson, K. and Willis, J. (2001). Paradigms and Frames in Distance Education: Toward Collaborative Electronic Learning, *International Journal of Educational Communication, 7* (3), 293-322.

Heinstorm, J. (2005). Fast Surfing, Broad Scanning and Deep Diving: The Influence of Personality and Study Approach on Students' Information-Seeking Behavior, *Journal of Documentation, 6* (2), 228-247.

Heppel, S. (1989). Digital Divide, *The Times Supplement,* 24 November, London.

Heyneman, S. P. and Haynes, K. T. (2004). International Uses of Education Technology: Threats and Opportunities. In: Chapman, D. W. and Mahlck, L. O. (Eds.), *Adapting Technology For School Improvement: A Global Perspective.* UNESCO: International Institute For Educational Planning, Paris.

Herrington, J. and Oliver, R. (2000). An Instructional Design Framework for Authentic Learning Environment, *Educational Technology Research and Development, 48* (3),23-38.

Hill. T. R. and Roldan, M. (2005). Toward Third Generation Threaded Discussions for Mobile Learning: Opportunities and Challenges for Ubiquitous Collaborative Environments, *Information Systems Frontiers, 7* (1), 55-70.

Hislop, G. and Ellis, H. (2004). A Study of Faculty Effort in Online Teaching, *Internet and Higher Education, 7* (1), 15-32.

Hilton, J. (2006). The Future of Higher Education: Sunrise or Perfect Storm? *EDUCAUSE Review 41* (2), 59-71.

Hiltz, S. R., Zhang, Y. and Turoff, M. (2001). *Studies of Effectiveness of Learning Networks.* Newark, N.J.: New Jersey Institute of Technology.

Ho, C. P. and Burniske, R. W. (2005). The Evolution of a Hybrid Classroom: Introducing Online Learning to Educators in American Samoa, *Tech Trends, 49* (1), 24-29.

Hogan, R. L. and Mcknight, M. A. (2007). Exploring Burnout among University Online Instructors, *Internet and Higher Education, 10* (2), 117-124

Hoffmann, S. (2005). *Building E-Learning Organizations,* Presented at the Online EDUCA Berlin Conference, 29 November- 2 December.

Holmberg, B. (1989). *Theory and Practice of Distance Education.* London: Routledge.

Holmberg, B. (2005). *The Evolution, Principles and Practices of Distance Education.* Oldenburg: Biliotheks_Und Informationssystem Der Universitatt Oldenburg.

Hong, L. (2008). Blending Online Components into Traditional Instruction in Pre-Service Teacher Education: The Good, the Bad, and the Ugly, *International Journal for the Scholarship of Teaching and Learning, 2* (1).

Howell, S., Williams, P. and Lindsay, N. (2003). Thirty-Two Trends Affecting Distance Education: An Informed Foundation for Strategic Planning, *Online Journal of Distance Learning Administration 6* (3).

Hulsmann, T. (2004). The Two-Pronged Attack on Learner Support: Costs and Centrifugal Forces of Convergence. In U. Bernath and A. Szcus (Eds.) *Supporting the Learner in Distance Education and E-Learning: Proceedings of the Third EDEN Research Workshop.* Oldenburg: Bibliotheks-Und-Informationssytem Der Universitaat Oldenburg, 498-504.

Immersive Education (2008). http://immersiveeducation.org

Institute for Higher Education Policy (2000). *Quality on the Line: Benchmarks for Success in Internet-Based Distance Education.* Washington, D. C.: National Education Association And Blackboard Inc.

Institute of International Education (2004). *Open Doors: Statistics on International Student Mobility*, IIE Network.

Jones, A. and Issrof, K. (2005). Learning Technologies: Affective and Social Issues in Computer-Supported Collaborative Learning, *Computers and Education, 44* (4), 395-408.

Jones, S. (2003). *Let the Games Begin: Gaming Technology and Entertainment among College Students.* Washington DC: Pew Internet and American Life Project.

Johnson, C. M. (2001). A Survey of Current Research on Online Communities of Practice, *Internet and Higher Education, 4* (1), 45-60.

Johnstone, J. and Baker, L. T. (2002). *Assessing the Impact of Technology on Teaching and Learning.* Ann Arbor: University of Michigan.

Jones, S. (2002). *The Internet Goes to College: How Students are Living in the Future with Today's Technology.* Washington, D.C.: Pew Internet and American Life Project.

Kanuka, H., Jugdev, K., Heller, R. and West, D. (2008). The Rise of the Teleworker: False Promises and Responsive Solutions, *Higher Education, 56* (2), 149-165.

Keegan, M. (1986). *The Foundations of Distance Education.* Beckenham: Croom Helm.

Keegan, M. (2000*). E-Learning: The Engine of The Knowledge Economy.* New York: Keegan.

Khan, B. H. (Ed.) (1997). *Web-Based Instruction*. New Jersey: Prentice Hall.

Kidd, T. and Chen, I. (Eds.) (2008). *Social Information Technology: Connecting Society and Cultural Issues.* Hershey, PA: Information Science Reference.

Kirk, E. and Bartelstein, A. (1999). Libraries Close in on Distance Education, *Library Journal, 124* (6).

Kozma, R. B. (Ed.) (2003). *Technology, Innovation, and Educational Change: A Global Perspective.* Eugene, Oregon: ISTE.

Kurtz, G. (2008). *Technological Innovation in Teaching at Bar-Ilan University: Transfer from Experimental Phase to Ongoing Adoption,* Paper presented at a Symposium on 'Attitudes of Academic Faculty towards the Implementation of Technologies in Teaching', Raanana: Open University of Israel, 31 March.

Lacritz, J. R. (2004). Exploring Burnout among University Faculty: Incidence, Performance, and Demographic Issues, *Teaching and Teacher Education, 20* (1), 713-729.

Lamont, I. (2008). *Virtual Reality and Higher Education: Another Perspective,* Terra Nova Blogs.

Ladner, B., Beagle, D., Steele, J. R. and Steele, L. (2004). Rethinking Online Instruction – From Content Transmission to Cognitive Immersion, *Reference and User Services Quarterly, 43* (4), 329-337.

Lapointe D. (2006). The Role of Transformational Learning in Distance Education: Becoming Aware. In: M. F. Beaudoin (Ed.) (2006). *Perspectives on Higher Education in the Digital Age.* New York: Nova Science, 91-110.

Laurillard, D. (2002). *Rethinking University Teaching: A Framework for the Effective Use of Learning Technologies.* London: Falmer Routledge, 2nd Edition.

Lenhart, A. (2003). *The Ever Shifting Internet Population: A New Look at Internet Access and the Digital Divide.* Washington DC: Pew Internet And American Life Project.

Lestz, M. (2005). Profs Without Borders: A Plan to Reconnect American Higher Education with the World, *Connection,* Fall 2005, 45-47.

Levin, D. and Arafeh, S. (2002). *The Digital Disconnect: The Widening Gap between Internet-Savvy Students and Their Schools.* Washington, D.C.: Pew Internetand American Life Project, 14 August.

Levy, D. (2008). *Private Higher Education's Global Surge: Emulating US Patterns?,* Paper presented at the Conference On 'Privatization In Higher Education', Haifa: Samuel Neeman Institute, The Technion.

Lewis, L., Snow, K., Farris, E., and Levin, D. (1999). *Distance Education at Postsecondary Education Institutions: 1997-98.* Washington, D.C.: US Department of Education, National Center for Educational Statistics.

Lindsey, M. (2003). *Copyright Law on Campus.* Washington State University Press.

Littleton, K. and Light, P. (Eds.) (1999). *Learning with Computers: Analysing Productive Interaction.* London: Routledge.

Losh, E. (2005). Virtual Politik: Obstacles to Building Virtual Communities in Traditional Institutions of Knowledge, Research and Occasional Paper Series: CSHE.9.05, UC Berkeley.

Lytras, M. D., Gasevic, D., Pablos and Huang, W. (Eds.) (2008). *Technology Enhanced Learning: Best Practices.* Hershey, PA: IGI Publishing.

Mack, R. L. (2001). *The Digital Divide: Standing at the Intersection of Race and Technology.* Durham, NC: Carolina Academic Press.

Mackintosh, W. (2006). Modeling Alternatives for Tomorrow's University: Has the Future Already Happened? In: M. F. Beaudoin, (Ed.) *Perspectives on Higher Education in the Digital Age.* New York: Nova Science, 111-136.

Martin, M. and Jennings, A. (2002). The Adoption, Diffusion and Exploitation of E-Learning in Europe: An Overview and Analysis of the UK, Germany and France. Dundee: University Of Abertay, Dundee Business School.

Martinez, M. C. (2004). *Meeting the Challenge of Population Growth and the Future Demand for Postsecondary Considerations for State Higher Education Policy.* Education Commission of The States.

Martyn, M. (2003). The Hybrid Online Model: Good Practice, *EDUCAUSE Quarterly, 23* (1), 18-23.

Masi, A. C. and Winer, L. R. (2005). A University-Wide Vision of Teaching and Leaning with Information Technologies, *Innovations in Education and Teaching International, 42* (2), 147-155.

Maslach, C., Jackson, S. and Leiter, M. (1996). *Maslach Burnout Inventory Manual,* Palo Alto, CA: Consulting Psychologists Press (3rd Edition)..

Maslach, C. and Leiter, M. (1997). *The Truth about Burnout: How Organizations Cause Personal Stress and What to Do About It.* San Francisco: Jossey-Bass Publishers.

Matkin, G. W. (2002). *The Whys and How of Online Education at UC: A Dean's Perspective,* UC Tltc News and Events.

Mckenzie, J. (2003). The True Cost of Ownership, *The Educational Technology Journal, 12* (7), March.

Mena, M. (Ed.) (2007). *Construyendo la Nueva Agenda dè la Educación a Distancia.* Ciudad De Buenos Aires: La Crujia Ediciones.

Middlehurst, R. (Ed.) (2000). *The Business of Borderless Education.* London: Committee Of Vice Chancellors and Principles.

Middlehurst, R. (2003). Competition, Collaboration and ICT: Challenges and Choices for Higher Education Institutions. In: M. Van Der Wende and M. Van Der Ven (Eds.). *The Use of ICT In Higher Education: A Mirror of Europe.* Utrecht: Lemma.

Mitrano, T. (2006). Incommon: Toward Building a Global University, *EDUCAUSE Review, 41* (2), 74-75.

Moe, M. and Blodgett, H. (2000). *The Knowledge Web.* New York: Merrill Lynch.

Motlik, S. (2008). Mobile Learning in Developing Nations, *International Review in Open and Distance Learning, 9* (2).

Moore, M.G. and Kearsley, G. (2005). *Distance Education: A Systems View.* Belmont, CA: Wadsworth (2nd Edition).

Morrison, T. R. (1992). *Learning, Change and Synergism: The Potential of Open Universities,* A paper presented at the Annual Asian Association of Open Universities, Seoul, Korea, September.

Nachmias, R. (2002). A Research Framework for the Study of a Campus-Wide Web-Based Academic Instruction Project, *Internet and Higher Education, 5,* 213-229.

Naismith, L., Lonsdale, P., Vavoula, G. and Sharples, M. (2005). *Literature Review in Mobile Technologies and Learning,* Report 11, Nesta Futurelab Series.

National Center for Education Statistics (2003). *Distance Education At Degree-Granting Postsecondary Institutions: 2000-2001.* Washington D.C.: US Department of Education.

Http://Ncs.Ed.Gov/Surveys/Peqis/Publications/200317/.

National Research Council (2002). *Preparing for the Revolution: Information Technology and the Future of the Research University.* Washington, D.C.: The National Academies Press.

National Research Council (2005). *How Students Learn: History, Mathematics and Science in the Classroom.* Committee on how People Learn, A Targeted Report for Teachers: Center for Studies on Behavior and Development.

National Staff Development Council (2001). *E-Learning for Educators-Implementing the Standards for Staff Development.* http://www.nsdc.org/connect/projects/e-learning.pdf

Natrins, L. (2004). *It Can Make a Difference if it is Fit for Purpose.* Learning and Skills Development Agency.

Neave, G. (Ed.) (2000). *The Universities' Responsibilities to Society: International Perspectives.* Oxford: Pergamon Press and International Association of Universities.

Newman, A., Yegin, C. and Gallagher, S. (2002). The Forecast, *University Business, 4* (10):25-32.

Newman, F., Couturier, L. and Scurry, J. (2004). *The Future of Higher Education: Rhetoric, Reality and the Risks of the Market.* San Francisco: Jossey-Bass.

Ninnes, P. and Hellsten, M. (Eds) (2005). *Internationalizing Higher Education: Critical Explorations of Pedagogy and Policy*. CERC Studies in Comparative Education, Vol. *16*.

Nipper, S. (1989). Third Genration Distance Learning and Computer Conferencing. In: R. Mason and A. Kaye (Eds.), *Mindweave: Communication, Computers and Distance Education.* Oxford: Pergamon Press, 63-73.

Noam, E. (1999). *Are the Cyber Universities the Future of Higher Education?*, Lecture presented at the Bruno Kreisky Forum for International Dialogue, Vienna, 10 June.

Noble, D. F. (2001). *Digital Diploma Mills: The Automation of Higher Education.* New York: Monthly Review Press.

Norris, P. (2001). *Digital Divide? Civic Engagement, Information Poverty, and the Internet Worldwide.* New York: Cambridge University Press.

Oblinger, D. (2003). Boomers, Gen-Xers, and Millennials: Understanding the New Students, *EDUCAUSE Review, 38* (4), 37-47.

Oblinger, D., Barone, C. and Hawkins, B. (2001). *Distributed Education and its Challenges: An Overview.* Washington, D. C.: American Council on Education for EDUCAUSE.

Oblinger, D. G. and Oblinger, J. L. (Eds.) (2005). *Educating the Net Generation.* Boulder, Co.: EDUCAUSE.

O'Brien, L. (2005). E-Research: An Imperative for Strengthening Institutional Partnerships, *EDUCASE Review, 40* (6).

OECD (2001). *Education Policy Analysis: Education and Skills.* Paris: Organization for Economic Cooperation and Development.

OECD (2004). *Internationalization and Trade in Higher Education: Opportunities and Challenges.* Paris: Organization for Economic Cooperation and Development.

OECD (2005). *E-Learning in Tertiary Education: Where Do We Stand?* Paris: Centre for Educational Research And Innovation.

Olsen, F. (2002). MIT's Open Window: Putting Course Materials Online - The University Faces High Expectations, *The Chronicle of Higher Education*, 6 December.

Oppenheimer, T. (2003). *The Flickering Mind: The False Promise of Technology in the Classroom and how Learning Can be Saved.* New York: Random House.

Ordorika, I. (2006). *Commitment to Society: Contemporary Challenges for Public Research Universities*, A paper presented at the UNESCO Colloquium on Research and Higher Education, Paris, 1 December.

Paul, R. (1990). *Open Learning and Open Management: Leadership and Integrity in Distance Education.* London: Kogan Page.

Paulson, K. (2002). Reconfiguring Faculty Roles for Virtual Settings, *Journal of Higher Education, 73* (1), 123-140.

Perraton, H. (2000). *Open and Distance Learning in the Developing World.* London: Routledge.

Peters, O. (1994). Distance Education and Industrial Production: A Comparative Interpretation in Outline. In M. Keegan (Ed.), *Otto Peters on Distance Education.* London: Routledge, 107-127

Peters, O. (1997). Fernuniversität. In: I. Mugridge (Ed.). *Founding the Open Universities.* New Delhi: Sterling Publishers, 53-79.

Peters, O. (2001). *Learning and Teaching in Distance Education: Analysis and Interpretations from an International Perspective.* London: Kogan Page.

Peters, O. (2004). *Distance Education in Transition: New Trends and Challenges.* Oldenburg: Bibliotheks-Und Informationssystem Der Universitat Oldenburg (4th Edition).

Petrides, L.A. (Ed.) (2000). *Case Studies on Information Technology in Higher Education: Implications for Policy and Practice.* Hershey, PA: Idea Group Publishing.

Pfeffer, T. (2003). *Virtualization of Research Universities: Raising the Right Questions to Address Key Functions of the Institution.* Research and Occasional Papers Series, CSHE 6.03, Berkeley: University of California at Berkeley.

Pines, A. (1993). Burnout: An Existential Perspective. In: W. B. Schaufeli, D. Maslach and T. Marek (Eds.). *Professional Burnout: Research Developments in Theory and Research.* Washington D. C.: Taylor and Francis.

Pittinsky, M. (2003). *The Wired Tower: Perspectives on the Impact of the Internet on Higher Education.* Upper Saddle River, N.J.: Financial Time and Prentice Hall.

Politis, D. (Ed.) (2008). *E-Learning Methodologies and Computer Applications in Archeology.* Hershey, PA: Information Science Reference.

Pollock, N. and Cornford, J. (2002). Theory and Practice of the Virtual University. *Ariadne, 24.*

Ponzurick, T. G., France, K. and Logar, C. M. (2000). Delivering Graduate Marketing Education: An Analysis of Face-To-Face versus Distance Education, *Journal of Marketing Education, 22* (3), 180-187.

Porter, P. and O'Connor, L. (2001). *What Makes Distance Learning Effective? Support Mechanisms to Maximize the Impact of Distance Learning in Higher Education.* Cambridge, MA: Mass Interaction.

Porto, S. and Berge, Z. L. (2008). Distance Education and Corporate Training in Brazil: Regulations and Interrelationships, *International Review of Research in Open and Distance Learning, 9* (2).

Postman, N. (1993). *The Surrender of Culture and Technology.* New York: Vintage Books.

Potashnik, M. and Adkins, D. (1996). *Cost Analysis of Information Technology Projects in Education: Experiences from Developing Countries.* Education and Technology Series, *1*, (3), Education Section, Human Development, World Bank.

Puzziferro-Schnitzer, M. (2005). Managing Virtual Adjunct Faculty: Applying the Seven Principles of Good Practice, *Online Journal of Distance Learning Administration, VIII* (2).

Qiu, J. and Thompson, E. (2007). Mobile Communication and Asian Modernities, *New Media and Society, 9* (6), 895-901.

Ramos, A., Trinona, J. and Lambert, D. (2006). Vialbility of SMS Technologies for Non-Formal Distance Education. In: J. Baggaley (Ed.), *Information and Communication Technology for Social Development.* Jakarta: ASEAN Foundation, 69-80.

Rasmussen, W. D. (1989). *Taking the University to the People: Seventy-Five Years of Cooperative Extension.* Ames: Iowa State University Press.

Roberston, R. (1992). *Globalisation.* London: Sage.

Robinson, S. and Guernsey, L. (1999). Microsoft and MIT To Launch I-Campus, *International Harold Tribune*, 6 October.

Ross, M. G. (1976). *The University: The Autonomy of Academe.* New York: Mcgraw Hill.

Rothblatt, S. (1997). *The Modern University and its Discontents: The Fate of Newman's Legacies in Britain and America.* Cambridge: University Press.

Rothblatt, S. (2007). *Education's Abiding Moral Dilemma: Merit and Worth in the Cross-Atlantic Democracies, 1800-2006.*Cambridge University Press: Symposium Books.

Rovai, A. P. (2004). A Constructivist Approach to Online College Learning, *Internet and Higher Education, 7* (2), 79-83.

Rovai, A. P. (2007). Facilitating Online Discussions Effectively, *Internet and Higher Education, 10* (1), 77-88.

Rovai, A. P., Ponton, M. K., Derrick, M. G. and Davis, J. M. (2006). Student Evaluation of Teaching in Virtual and Traditional Classrooms: A Comparative Analysis, *Internet and Higher Education, 9* (1), 23-35.

Rumble, G. (2001). Just How Relevant Is E-Education to Global Education Needs?, *Open Learning, 16* (3), 223-232.

Russell, T.L. (2001). *The No Significant Difference Phenomenon: A Comparative Research Annotated Bibliography on Technology for Distance Education.* Raleigh, NC: North Carolina State University.

Ryan, Y. (2002). *Emerging Indicators of Success and Failure in Borderless Higher Education.* London: A Report for The Observatory on Borderless Higher Education.

Saba, F. (2006). The New Academy: A Dynamic Vision for a Postmodern Era of Distance Education. In: M. F. Beaudoin (Ed.) (2006). *Perspectives on Higher Education in the Digital Age,* New York: Nova Science, 259-276.

Schachter, L., Pence, A., Zuckernick, A. and Roberts, J. (2006). Distance Learning in Africa. In: M. Beaudoin (Ed.), *Perspectives on Higher Education in the Digital Age,* New York: Nova Science, 165-186.

Schell, G. P. (2004). Universities Marginalize Online Courses, *Communication of The ACM, 47* (7).

Schlusmans, K., Koper, R. and Giesbertz, W. (2004). Work Processes for the Development of Integrated E-learning Courses. In: W. Jochems, J. Van Merrienboer and R. Koper (Eds.), *Integrated E-learning: Implications for Pedagogy, Technology and Organization.* London: RoutledgeFalmer.

Schramm, R. M., Wagner, R. J. and Werner, J. M. (2001). *Students' Perceptions of the Effectiveness of Web-based Courses*, Madison WI: Magna Publications.

Scott, H., Chenette, J. and Swartz, J. (2002). The Integration of Technology into Learning and Teaching in Liberal Arts, *Liberal Education,* Spring 2002, 30-35.

Scott, L. H., Laws, R. D., Williams P. B. and Lindsay, N. K. (2006). Trends Affecting Higher Education and Distance Learning. In: M. F. Beaudoin (Ed.) (2006). *Perspectives on Higher Education in the Digital Age,* New York: Nova Science, 227-246.

Selinger, M. and Pearson, J. (Eds.) (1999). *Telematics in Education: Trends and Issues,* Oxford: Pergamon Press.

Selwyn, N. (2003). *Understanding Students' (Non) Use of Information and Communication Technology in University.* Cardiff University: School of Social Sciences.

Sewart, D. (1992). Mass Higher Education: Where Are We Going?, In: G. E. Ortner , K. Graff and H. Wilmersdoerfer (Eds.), *Distance Education as Two-Way Communication: Essays in Honour of Borje Holmberg.* Frankfurt: Peter Lang, 229-239.

Shea, P., Sau-Li, C. and Pickett, A. (2006). A Study of Teaching Presence and Student Sense of Learning Community in Fully Online and Web-

Enhanced College Courses, *Internet and Higher Education, 9* (3), 175-190.

Shearer, R. L. and Chakiris, H. L. (2006). Educational Access and the Role of Distance Education. In: M. F. Beaudoin, (Ed.) (2006). *Perspectives on Higher Education in the Digital Age.* New York: Nova Science, 49-62.

Siemens, G. (2004). *Connectivism: A Learning Theory for the Digital Age,* December 12.
http:///www.elearnspace.org/articles/connectivism.htm

Sikora, A. C. and Carroll, C. D. (2002). *Postsecondary Education Descriptive Analysis Reports* (NCES 2003-154). Washington D. C.: US Department of Education, National Center for Education Statistics.

Somekh, B. and Davis, N. (Eds.) (1997). *Using Information Technology Effectively in Teaching and Learning.* London: Routledge.

South African Institute of Distance Education (2004). *Costing Distance and Open Learning in Sub-Saharan Africa,* Commonwealth of Learning.

Stanford University (2002). *Stanford Facts.* Stanford: Stanford University Press.

Stephenson, J. (Ed.) (2001). *Teaching and Learning Online: Pedagogies for New Technologies.* London: Kogan Page.

Strijbos, J. W., Martens, R. L. and Jochems, W. M. G. (2004). Designing the Interaction: Six Steps to Designing Computer-Supported Ground-Based Learning, *Computers and Education, 42* (4), 403-424.

Tait, A. and Mills, R. (Eds.) (2003). *Rethinking Learner Support in Distance Education: Change and Continuity in an International Context.* London: Routledge Falmer.

Tanner, M. R. (1999). *Testimony before Representatives of the United States Copyright Office,* February 10, Los Angeles, CA.

Taylor, P. A. and Harris, J. (2005). *Digital Concepts: The Cultural Context of New Information Technologies.* London: Routledge.

Thornton, P. and Houser, C. (2004). *Using Mobile Phones in Education.* 2nd IEE International Workshop on Wireless and Mobile Technologies in Education.

Tifflin, J. and Rajasingham, L. (1995). *In Search of the Virtual Classroom: Education in an Information Society.* London: Routledge.

Tilak, J. B. G. (2008). *Current Trends in Private Higher Education in Asia,* Paper presented at the Conference on 'Privatization In Higher Education', Haifa: Samuel Neeman Institute, The Technion.

Todd, R. L. and Edmonds C. D. (2006). Building Walls or Building Bridges: Accessibility of Online Education. In: M. F. Beaudoin (Ed.) (2006). *Perspectives on Higher Education in the Digital Age.* New York: Nova Science, 207-226.

Toffler, A. (1980) *The Third Wave.* New York: William Morrow.

Trow, M. (1999). Lifelong Learning through the New Information Technologies, *Higher Education Policy, 12* (2), 201-217.

Trow, M. (2001). *From Mass Higher Education to Universal Access: The American Advantage.* Research and Occasional Papers Series: CSHE 1.00, Berkeley: University Of California.

Trucano, M. (2005). *Knowledge Maps: Icts in Education.* Washington D.C.: Infodev. World Bank: The Information for Development Program.

Twigg, C. (2001) *Innovations in Online Learning: Moving beyond the No Significant Difference.* Troy, NY: Rensselaer Polytechnic Institute, Center for Academic Transformation, Pew Learning and Technology Program.

Twigg, C. (2004). A Little Knowledge is a Dangerous Thing, *The Learning Market Space,* Section 1, July 4. The Center for Academic Transformation.

UNESCO (2002). *Consultative Workshop for Developing Performance Indicators for ICT in Education.* Manila, The Philippines, 28-30 August.

UNESCO (2003). *Developing and Using Indicators of ICT In Education.*Paris: UNESCO.

UNESCO (2005). *ICT in Education: Policy Makers Toolkit.* Bangkok: Author.

University of Phoenix (2008). http://www.phoenix.edu

US Department of Education (2002). *A Profile of Participation in Distance Education: 1999-2000.* Washington D.C.: National Center for Educational Statistics, NCES 2003-154.

van Der Molen, H. J. (Ed.) (2001) Virt*ual University? Educational Environments of the Future.* London: Portland Press Ltd.

van Der Wende, M. C. (2001). Internationalisation Policies: About New Trends and Constraining Paradigms, *Higher Education Policy, 14* (2), 249-259.

van Der Wende, M.C. (2002). *The Role of US Higher Education in the Global E-learning Market.* Research and Occasional Papers Series. UC Berkeley: Center for Studies in Higher Education, 1.02.

Veen, W. (2005). *2020 Visions,* Presented at the Online EDUCA Berlin Conference, 29 November- 2 December.

Vest, C. M. (2001). *Disturbing the Educational Universe: Universities in The Digital Age – Dinosaurs or Prometheans?* Report of the President for the Academic Year 2000-01, MIT New Office.

Vest, C. M. (2004). Why MIT Decided to Give Away all its Course Materials via the Internet? *Chronicle of Higher Education*, January 30.

Vest, C. M. (2007). *The American Research University from World War II to World Wide Web.* Berkeley: University of California Press.

Vincent-Lancrin, S. (2004). *Building Capacity through Cross-Border Tertiary Education,* Paper prepared for the UNESCO/OECD Australia Forum on Trade in Educational Services, Sydney, Australia.

Visser, J. (2006). Universities, Wisdom, Transdisciplinarity and the Challenges and Opportunities of Technology. In: M. Beaudoin (Ed.), *Perspectives on Higher Education in the Digital Age.* New York: Nova Science, 187-205.

Visser, L. and West, P. (2005). The Promise of M-Learning for Distance Education in South Africa and Other Developing Nations. In: Y. Visser, L. Visser, M. Simonson and R. Amirault (Eds.). *Trends and Issues in Distance Education: International Perspectives.* Greenwich, CT: Information Age Publishing, 117-129.

Vrasidas, C. (2000). Constructivism versus Objectivism: Implications for Interaction, Course Design, and Evaluation in Distance Education, *International Journal of Educational Telecommunications, 6*(4), 339-362.

Vrasidas, C. and Glass, G. V. (Eds.) (2002). *Distance Education and Distributed Learning.* Greenwich, CT: Information Age Publishing.

Vrasidas, C. and Mcisaac, M. S. (1999). Factors Influencing Interaction in an Online Course, *American Journal of Distance Education, 13* (3), 22-36.

Wagner, D., Day, B. and Sun, J. S. (2004). *Information Technologies and Education for the Poor in Africa,* UK Department for International Development.

Wagschal, P. H. (1998). Distance Education Comes to the Academy: But are we Asking the Right Questions?, *Internet and Higher Education, 1* (2), 125-130.

Wallace, R. M. (2004). A Framework for Understanding Teaching with the Internet, *American Educational Research Journal, 41* (2), 447-488.

Warschauer, M. (2003). *Technology and Social Inclusion: Rethinking the Digital Divide.* Cambridge, MA: MIT Press.

Washburn, J. (2005). *University, Inc.: The Corporate Corruption of American Higher Education,* Basic Books.

Weiler, H., Guri-Rosenblit, S. and Sawyerr, A. (2008). Universities as Centers of Research and Knowledge Creation: An Endangered Species? - Summary Report. In: H. Vessuri and U. Teichler (Eds.), *Universities as Centers of Research and Knowledge Creation: An Endangered Species?* Dordrecht: Sense Publishers, 15-32.

Welch, A. (Ed.) (2005). *The Professoriate: Profile of a Profession.* Dordrecht: Springer.

Western Governors University (2008). http://www.elearners.com/college/wgu

Williams, P. E. (2003). Roles and Competencies for Distance Education Programs in Higher Education Institutions, *American Journal of Distance Education, 17* (1), 45-57.

Wilson, B. G. (2001). *Trends and Futures of Education: Implications for Distance Education*, Carbo: Cudevner.

Wilson, B. C., Ludwig-Hardman, S., Thornam, C. and Dunlap, J. C. (2004). Bounded Community: Designing and Facilitating Learning Communities in Formal Courses, *The International Review of Research in Open and Distance Learning, 5* (3).

Wilson, J. M. (2002). *E-Learning: Is It Over?* http://www.umassoline.net/news/shownews/cfm?news_id=23

Winston, B. E. (2006). A Future Scenario of Education as a Result of The Digital Age, In: M. F. Beaudoin (Ed.) (2006). *Perspectives on Higher Education in The Digital Age,* New York: Nova Science, 277-292.

Wong, K. and Sayo, P. (2004). *Free Open Source Software: A General Introduction,* UNDP-APDIP.

Woo, Y. and Reeves, T. C. (2007). Meaningful Interaction in Web-based Learning: A Social Constructivist Interpretation, *Internet and Higher Education, 10* (1), 15-25.

Wood, T. and Mccarthy, C. (2004). *Understanding and Preventing Teacher Burnout.* Washington, D.C.: Office of Educational Research and Improvement.

World Bank (2000). *Higher Education in Developing Countries: Peril and Promise,* Task Force on Higher Education and Society.

World Bank (2002a). *Constructing Knowledge Societies: New Challenges for Tertiary Education.* Washington D.C.: Directions in Development.

World Bank (2002b). *The World of ICT In Education: A Seminar for Policymakers* http://www.worldbank.org/wbi/ictforeducation.html/policymakers.html

Wyckoff, A. and Schaper, M. (2005). *The Changing Dynamics of the Global Market for the Highly Skilled,* Prepared for Advancing Knowledge and the Knowledge Economy Conference, At the National Academy of Science, Washington, D.C., 10-11 January.

Xebec Mcgraw and Training Magazine (2001) *Corporate E-Learning: Realizing the Potential,* 2 October.

Zemsky, R. and Massy, W. F. (2004a). *Thwarted Innovation: What Happened to E-learning and Why,* A Final Report for 'The Weatherstation Project' of the Learning Alliance at the University of Pennsylvania in Cooperation with the Thomson Corporation. University of Pennsylvania: The Learning Alliance for Higher Education.

Zemsky, R. and Massy, W. F. (2004b). Why the E-learning Boom Went Bust?, *The Chronicle of Higher Education, 50* (40), B.6-B.8

Zemsky, R. and Massy, W. F. (2005). Stalled: E-learning as a Thwarted Innovation. In: A. A. Carr-Chellman (Ed.) (2005). *Global Perspectives on E-Learning.* Thousands Oaks: Sage Publications, .

Zhang, D., Zhao, J. L., Zhou, L. and Nunamaker, J. F. (2004). Can E-learning Replace Classroom Learning? *Communications of the ACM, 47* (5).

INDEX

A

academic settings, 16, 17
academics, 20, 21, 22, 28, 48, 49, 52, 71, 84, 88, 94, 107, 117, 132, 133
access, 6, 33, 34, 38, 51, 55, 58, 59, 63, 70, 71, 72, 73, 75, 76, 78, 79, 82, 93, 94, 99, 101, 107, 108, 118, 119, 120, 121, 125, 129, 135, 137
accessibility, 77, 120
accounting, 90
accreditation, 115
acculturation, 56
acquisition of knowledge, 48
adaptation, 43, 47, 52, 53, 54, 59
administrators, 28
adult education, 41
adult population, 87
adults, 43, 87, 107, 128
advertisements, 73
aesthetics, 96
Africa, 74, 75, 76, 77, 120, 137, 151, 161, 162, 164
age, 11, 17, 48, 50, 52, 57, 124
aging, 66
agriculture, 84
alienation, 28
alternative, 4, 6, 36, 124, 134
aluminium, 66
ambiguity, 3, 4, 28
animations, 56
anxiety, 56, 119
argument, 29, 96, 98
Armenia, 115
articulation, 116
artificial intelligence, 10
Asia, 9, 77, 140, 143, 148, 149, 162
assault, 119
assessment, 19
assimilation, 44
assumptions, 19, 47, 52, 55, 60
asynchronous communication, 32
attitudes, 24, 56, 80, 91
Australia, 9, 24, 39, 80, 81, 126, 143, 144, 151, 164
automation, 63
autonomy, 21, 82, 114, 115
availability, 95
Azerbaijan, 115

B

banking, 89, 111
bankruptcy, 112
barriers, 11, 12, 40, 50, 52, 74, 80, 100
behaviorism, 60
beliefs, 106, 124

Bell R., 18
benchmarks, 17, 31
beverages, 89
bias, 5, 110
biotechnology, 117
birth, 102, 120
Bologna Process, 82, 83, 115, 116
brain, 74
brain drain, 74
Brazil, 9, 71, 89, 143, 159
Britain, 72, 78, 79, 160
broadcast media, 8
Burkina Faso, 74
burning, 25, 132
burnout, 26, 27, 28
business education, 88
business environment, 85
business model, 64

C

calculus, 53
Cambridge University, 17
Canada, 9, 30, 70, 76, 78, 116, 126, 140
capitalism, 90
cast, 106
cell, 2, 77
cell phones, 77
channels, 126
childhood, 76
children, 12
Chile, 74
China, 71, 72, 73, 77, 81, 87, 105, 111, 148
circulation, 119
civil servants, 84
class size, 63
classes, 10, 13, 19, 28, 32, 33, 48, 50, 54, 57, 87, 93, 108, 119, 126, 127, 135
classification, 57
classroom, 5, 8, 10, 19, 20, 21, 22, 29, 36, 38, 44, 56, 63, 64, 91, 95, 119, 129, 135
classrooms, 2, 6, 7, 32, 48, 52, 67, 87, 91
closure, 72
cognition, 59
cognitive psychology, 60
cohesion, 50
cohort, 76, 124
collaboration, 23, 32, 73, 79, 84, 86, 101, 104, 106, 113, 114, 115, 116, 131, 137
colleges, 3, 7, 19, 25, 39, 44, 51, 52, 62, 64, 66, 75, 89, 102, 114, 116, 124, 125, 134, 137
commerce, 1, 70
commodity, 51, 80, 82, 116
communication, 1, 2, 3, 5, 6, 8, 10, 15, 21, 23, 28, 31, 32, 36, 37, 41, 45, 47, 50, 56, 60, 69, 70, 71, 73, 79, 81, 91, 93, 96, 97, 98, 114, 126, 129, 131, 132, 134, 135, 136
communication skills, 15
communication technologies, 1, 2, 6, 8, 10, 31, 37, 41, 45, 47, 69, 71, 73, 81, 91, 93, 114, 126, 131, 134
community, 11, 20, 23, 25, 27, 30, 89, 109, 119, 121, 125, 131, 132, 136, 138
competence, 25, 33
competency, 127
competition, 101, 104, 109, 113, 114, 116
competitive advantage, 114
competitiveness, 80, 83
complement, 25, 38, 42, 64, 132
complexity, 5, 78, 103, 106
components, 19, 39, 57, 128
composition, 8, 124
comprehension, 60
computer conferencing, 31, 108
computer skills, 90
computer-mediated communication (CMC), 2
computing, 136
concentrates, 88, 90
concentration, 22
conception, 18
conceptual model, 134
confidence, 25, 133
conflict, 27
confusion, 4, 6, 56, 58
connectivity, 31, 75, 76, 77, 131
consciousness, 103

construction, 60, 61
consumers, 62
consumption, 54
control, 5, 22, 55, 118, 119
convergence, 115, 116
copper, 66
corporate sector, 86
corporations, 64, 86, 89, 92, 110, 127, 128
correlations, 27
cost saving, 64
Costa Rica, 71
costs, 28, 62, 63, 64, 65, 66, 77, 85, 89, 93, 95, 96, 133
course content, 112
course work, 10
creativity, 15, 97, 98, 107
credibility, 77
credit, 51, 75, 85
critical thinking, 57
cultural norms, 79
cultural values, 82
culture, 11, 21, 38, 59, 78, 84, 86, 87, 106, 109, 110, 120, 123, 125, 135
curiosity, 62
curriculum, 75, 76, 78, 88
curriculum development, 75
customers, 53
cyberspace, 2
cycles, 129

D

danger, 73
data collection, 134
decision makers, 24, 131
decision making, 24, 54, 60, 85
decisions, 85, 99, 101
definition, 8, 54
delivery, 4, 5, 6, 9, 10, 21, 25, 39, 40, 41, 53, 56, 62, 63, 65, 66, 81, 89, 104, 108, 126, 130, 131
demand, 43, 49, 64, 65, 72, 75, 78, 83, 89, 95, 109, 111, 124
Democratic Party, 105
Denmark, 125
depersonalization, 27, 28
designers, 132, 134
desire, 97, 103, 120, 130
developed countries, 69, 76, 90, 91, 106, 107, 124
developing countries, 36, 39, 40, 66, 70, 71, 73, 74, 75, 76, 77, 89, 90, 91, 94, 104, 106, 108, 112, 121, 136, 138
differentiation, 22
diffusion, 77
digital divide, 73, 74, 76
digital technologies, 1, 2, 3, 4, 5, 6, 7, 9, 10, 13, 15, 16, 17, 20, 23, 24, 26, 28, 31, 32, 33, 34, 35, 37, 38, 40, 41, 42, 43, 44, 47, 48, 50, 51, 52, 54, 55, 57, 59, 60, 62, 65, 66, 69, 70, 73, 74, 75, 76, 78, 80, 82, 86, 90, 92, 93, 95, 96, 97, 101, 103, 105, 108, 114, 117, 123, 125, 129, 131, 132, 133, 134, 135, 137
disappointment, 86
discipline, 18, 97
disclosure, 117
discourse, 1, 2, 3, 5, 16, 59, 86
distance education, 5, 6, 7, 8, 9, 10, 11, 12, 13, 16, 21, 37, 39, 44, 45, 49, 50, 51, 52, 56, 63, 64, 66, 71, 74, 75, 77, 80, 89, 93, 94, 95, 96, 114, 124
distance learning, 2, 3, 5, 9, 12, 75, 81, 129
distribution, 118, 119
diversity, 69, 90, 110, 116, 124
division, 21, 63, 111
division of labor, 63
doctors, 17
donations, 84, 86
doors, 58
duplication, 67, 95, 115

E

East Asia, 120
Eastern Europe, 120, 126
economic development, 130
economic ideology, 103
economics, 65, 84, 97

education, 6, 7, 12, 16, 30, 37, 39, 44, 47, 48, 51, 56, 69, 70, 80, 81, 83, 94, 103, 106, 109, 111, 112, 116, 137, 139, 140, 141, 142, 143, 144, 145, 146, 147, 148, 149, 150, 151, 152, 153, 154, 155, 156, 157, 158, 159, 160, 161, 162, 163, 164, 165, 166
educational policy, 75
educational practices, 4
educational research, 30
educational services, 102, 109
educational settings, 2, 3, 4, 5, 6, 42, 43
egalitarianism, 105
elderly, 74
e-learning, 1, 2, 3, 4, 5, 6, 7, 8, 9, 10, 13, 20, 23, 29, 36, 38, 40, 43, 47, 50, 52, 53, 55, 56, 62, 63, 64, 65, 66, 70, 71, 76, 77, 89, 90, 93, 94, 98, 107, 108, 111, 112, 123, 129, 134, 157
electricity, 70
elementary school, 58
email, 32
emotional exhaustion, 27, 28
employees, 86, 88
employment, 2, 104, 124, 128, 130
encryption, 119
energy, 34
engagement, 30
England, 18, 112, 143
enrollment, 5, 54, 78, 81, 103, 112
enthusiasm, 53, 58
entrepreneurs, 53, 72, 111
entrepreneurship, 84
environment, 2, 3, 18, 24, 28, 29, 34, 57, 60, 61, 62, 106, 108, 114, 119, 135
epistemology, 59, 60
equality, 95
equity, 74, 76, 107, 108, 113
euphoria, 15
Euro, 150
Europe, 9, 17, 21, 70, 82, 83, 102, 115, 116, 144, 147, 150, 155, 156
European Commission, 104, 141, 148
European Union, 115, 116
exaggeration, 123
examinations, 5, 13, 18, 129
expenditures, 23, 43
expert teacher, 58, 59, 61, 91
expertise, 11, 19, 20, 53, 87, 106, 107
exports, 80

F

face-to-face interaction, 19, 91
failure, 3, 35, 44, 78, 112
fair use, 118, 119
fairness, 27
family, 11, 12, 60, 128
fatigue, 27
fear, 118
feedback, 23, 28, 31, 33, 35, 56, 61, 132
feelings, 23, 28, 56
financial resources, 91
Finland, 24, 39, 125
firms, 48, 105
first generation, 137
flexibility, 10, 12, 39, 43, 106, 107, 128, 129, 133, 135
flight, 64
focusing, 3, 18, 102, 130
France, 9, 82, 84, 155, 159
freedom, 18, 21, 22, 88, 126
frustration, 56
funding, 40, 48, 70, 75, 76, 82, 84, 97, 102, 113, 121
funds, 23, 52, 72, 73, 84, 105

G

General Accounting Office, 140
General Agreement on Trade in Services, 80
generation, 7, 54, 55, 57, 63, 110, 131
Georgia, 115
Germany, 9, 21, 24, 39, 79, 82, 84, 105, 155
global economy, 90, 105
global markets, 115

globalization, 101, 102, 103, 104, 106, 107, 110, 121
goals, 3, 41, 42, 54, 55, 66, 69, 83, 85, 86, 89, 92, 115
gold, 66
governance, 90, 134
government, 18, 43, 70, 72, 73, 75, 78, 80, 81, 83, 84, 96, 102, 105, 109, 112, 113, 114, 116, 117, 127
government budget, 113
government intervention, 83
grades, 23, 132
grading, 129
graduate students, 12, 97, 105
grass, 88
group work, 32, 61
groups, 9, 13, 19, 32, 33, 37, 39, 43, 73, 96, 107, 128
growth, 76, 89, 121
growth rate, 89
guidance, 56, 58, 61
guilty, 108
Gunawardena G. N., 21, 132

H

handheld devices, 10
hands, 35, 55
harmonization, 82
hazardous materials, 66
health, 12, 87
health care, 87
hegemony, 47, 120
high school, 130, 138
higher education, 2, 4, 6, 7, 8, 10, 12, 13, 15, 16, 17, 19, 20, 24, 26, 27, 30, 31, 36, 37, 38, 39, 41, 43, 44, 45, 47, 48, 50, 51, 52, 54, 55, 57, 59, 61, 62, 63, 64, 66, 69, 70, 72, 74, 75, 78, 79, 80, 81, 82, 83, 84, 86, 88, 89, 90, 92, 94, 96, 101, 102, 103, 104, 105, 106, 107, 108, 109, 110, 112, 113, 114, 115, 116, 119, 120, 121, 123, 124, 125, 126, 128, 130, 132, 133, 134, 135, 137
homework, 8, 13
hospitals, 12
host, 53, 74, 112
hotels, 89
house, 158
households, 74
human capital, 92, 96
human resources, 76
Humboldtian idea, 18
hybrid, 2, 48, 49, 130
hypermedia, 10

I

identity, 106
imagination, 58
immigration, 74
implementation, 5, 13, 24, 29, 35, 37, 40, 41, 42, 43, 47, 52, 53, 62, 66, 69, 70, 76, 78, 86, 93, 101, 123, 134
incentives, 23, 25, 48, 54, 81, 82, 132
income, 74
India, 71, 72, 73, 87, 90, 105
indicators, 42
individual rights, 30
individual students, 18
induction, 65
industrial revolution, 135
industry, 10, 48, 53, 84
infinite, 1
information processing, 55
information retrieval, 3, 5, 10, 96
information technology, 57, 71, 96, 134
infrastructure, 5, 16, 23, 40, 64, 65, 69, 70, 72, 73, 74, 76, 82, 89, 90, 92, 93, 95, 96, 100, 105, 111
initiation, 16
innovation, 3, 35, 36, 78, 88, 90, 135
insight, 115, 123
institutional infrastructure, 35
institutions, 4, 6, 7, 9, 10, 11, 12, 15, 16, 20, 23, 24, 25, 26, 31, 37, 39, 40, 43, 44, 45, 49, 50, 51, 54, 57, 59, 62, 66, 69, 70, 72, 73, 74, 75, 76, 80, 81, 82, 84, 86, 87, 88, 89, 90, 91, 92, 93, 96, 97, 101, 102, 103, 104, 106, 109, 111,

113, 114, 115, 116, 119, 121, 124, 125, 126, 127, 128, 129, 130, 132, 135, 137
instruction, 8, 20, 22, 26, 43, 49, 53, 56, 59, 70, 79, 93, 96, 98, 129, 133
instructional activities, 62
instructional design, 21, 22, 25, 27, 61, 99, 132
instructors, 10, 23, 24, 27, 28, 33, 135
integration, 24, 76, 78, 98
intellectual capital, 111
intellectual property, 29, 30, 54, 86, 101, 117, 118, 120
intellectual property rights, 29, 30, 54
intelligent systems, 98
intensity, 78, 96, 115
interaction, 2, 4, 5, 9, 26, 30, 32, 33, 48, 49, 50, 60, 61, 63, 64, 91, 93, 94, 99, 126, 131, 132
interactions, 32, 34, 60, 61, 62
international law, 83
international trade, 80
internationalization, 82, 102, 103, 106
interrelations, 17, 20, 29, 30, 59, 84, 101
intervention, 42, 61, 84
interview, 88
inventions, 117
investment, 43, 89, 106, 109, 111, 112
investors, 111
IP address, 119
isolation, 23, 27, 28, 56
Israel, 48, 49, 149, 151, 154
Italy, 82, 125

J

Japan, 9, 116, 136
job satisfaction, 28
jobs, 110
Johnstone B., 124
joint ventures, 64, 72, 85, 110
jurisdiction, 80, 104
justice, 87
justification, 79

K

kindergarten, 8, 13, 58, 137
knowledge economy, 43, 73
knowledge-based economy, 71
Korea, 77, 156

L

labour, 21, 93
lack of control, 27
land, 83
language, 1, 2, 80, 96
Latin America, 9, 120, 140
law suits, 86
laws, 66, 117, 118, 120
leadership, 36, 43, 44, 76, 81, 131
leadership style, 43
learners, 13, 15, 16, 23, 39, 43, 60, 61, 62, 70, 75, 76, 85, 99, 108, 129, 130, 132
learning, 2, 3, 4, 5, 6, 7, 8, 9, 10, 11, 13, 15, 16, 17, 18, 19, 20, 21, 22, 23, 24, 25, 26, 27, 28, 29, 30, 31, 32, 33, 34, 35, 36, 37, 38, 39, 40, 41, 42, 43, 44, 49, 50, 51, 53, 55, 56, 59, 60, 61, 63, 64, 65, 66, 70, 76, 77, 82, 85, 87, 89, 90, 94, 95, 96, 97, 99, 100, 104, 107, 114, 124, 125, 127, 128, 129, 130, 132, 133, 134, 135, 136, 137, 139, 141, 142, 161, 163, 166
learning behavior, 55
learning environment, 2, 40, 61, 62, 100
learning outcomes, 30
learning process, 8, 15, 19, 36, 39, 40, 42, 55, 70
learning styles, 35, 40, 128
legislation, 30
Lernfreiheit, 18
lesson plan, 25
licenses, 105
life cycle, 128
lifelong learning, 128, 130
limitation, 133
links, 10, 72, 84, 97, 104, 109

listening, 33
literacy, 13, 20, 54
loans, 5, 72
loneliness, 93
love, 56

M

Mackintosh, 2, 6, 7, 16, 19, 65, 134, 155
magazines, 135
Malaysia, 71, 111
management, 10, 11, 15, 16, 21, 22, 27, 37, 60, 64, 65, 75, 87, 90, 96, 115, 129, 130, 135
manpower, 120
marginal costs, 93
market, 44, 49, 53, 62, 71, 72, 78, 81, 82, 83, 85, 88, 89, 102, 103, 105, 107, 109, 110, 111, 112, 118, 119, 120, 130
market economy, 109
market position, 44
market share, 109
marketing, 5, 81, 88
markets, 15, 43, 50, 62, 102, 103, 109, 110, 113, 114
mass communication, 79
mass media, 79
mathematics, 96
maturation, 60
meanings, 1, 3, 60, 61
measures, 22, 28, 41, 119
media, 3, 7, 8, 9, 10, 13, 37, 41, 48, 50, 52, 55, 59, 71, 79, 96, 98, 99, 100, 107, 111, 118, 120, 121, 123, 124, 128, 133, 136, 137
memorizing, 33
memory, 60, 85
men, 17
mentoring, 28
messages, 56
meta-analysis, 30, 41
Mexico, 9, 106, 116, 141
Microsoft, 86, 92, 110, 149, 160
Middle East, 73, 120
minorities, 74
minority, 40, 53
missions, 63
misunderstanding, 3, 64
mobile phone, 77, 136
mobility, 10, 135
modeling, 98
models, 6, 38, 44, 71, 112, 117, 119, 136
modernity, 77
modules, 85
mold, 44
momentum, 117, 137
money, 54, 64, 85, 105
moral judgment, 96
motivation, 20, 103
movement, 30, 59, 60, 114, 117, 120, 121
multimedia, 129, 136
multinational companies, 105
music, 55, 56, 57

N

nanotechnology, 117
nation, 10, 102, 109
nation states, 102
National Center for Education Statistics, 51, 142, 157, 162
National Research Council, 10, 47, 98, 131, 134, 157
natural sciences, 98
neglect, 66
negotiating, 109
negotiation, 29
nerve, 58
Netherlands, 24, 39
network, 29, 77, 120, 131
networking, 106
New Zealand, 9
newspapers, 10
next generation, 137
Nobel Prize, 104
nonverbal signals, 32
North America, 9, 70, 77, 116, 120, 141
North American Free Trade Agreement, 116
Norway, 24, 39, 125

nursing, 87

O

objectification, 22
objectivity, 98
obligation, 18
observations, 98
oceans, 125
online learning, 2, 5, 13, 23, 25, 39, 42, 43, 44, 50, 53, 56, 64, 65, 80, 89, 96, 118, 129
openness, 27, 115, 121
optimism, 123
organization, 11, 16, 22, 35, 67, 78, 82, 87, 88, 100, 115, 116, 120, 135
Organization for Economic Cooperation and Development (OECD), 2, 7, 9, 10, 12, 16, 20, 21, 23, 25, 37, 38, 40, 49, 50, 62, 63, 64, 65, 66, 70, 74, 83, 97, 103, 104, 107, 121, 125, 135, 158, 164
organizational culture, 85
organizations, 4, 73, 89, 109, 115, 134, 138
orientation, 87, 97, 109
overload, 17, 26, 59
ownership, 29, 121
Oxbridge tradition, 18
Oxford University, 17

P

Pacific, 9, 81, 120, 143, 148, 149
Pakistan, 140
paradigm shift, 13, 16, 44
parents, 18
partnership, 79
passive, 60
patents, 105, 117
Paul R., 115
pedagogy, 10, 26, 36, 41, 128
peer group, 23
peers, 48, 56
penalties, 119
perceptions, 56, 85
personal accomplishment, 27, 28
personal computers, 16, 121
personal learning, 53
Peters O., 19, 21
pharmacology, 117
Philippines, 136, 163
physics, 98
planning, 5, 21, 51, 63, 67, 75, 77
Plato, 11
policy makers, x, 6, 15, 24, 41, 54, 71, 101, 123
politics, 1
pools, 103
poor, 27, 75, 77, 90, 100, 138
population, 49, 70, 74, 121, 137
portfolio, 33
post-secondary institutions, 12
power, 88, 92
predictability, 98
prediction, 123
preference, 112, 126
president, 21, 51, 79, 102
pressure, 65, 102, 130
prestige, 87
prices, 119
primacy, 103, 131
prisons, 12
privacy, 119
private enterprises, 105
private sector, 72, 89, 116, 130
privatization, 109
problem solving, 15, 31, 56, 57, 60, 97
producers, 21, 109, 120, 121, 132
production, 3, 4, 5, 21, 22, 63, 95, 97, 99, 127, 132
productivity, 89
professional careers, 107
professional development, 25
professions, 17, 124
profit, 51, 57, 62, 63, 64, 65, 66, 72, 73, 78, 86, 87, 88, 89, 90, 104, 110, 111, 114, 127
profitability, 103
profits, 62, 124

program, 3, 7, 10, 12, 18, 26, 49, 62, 76, 90, 127, 129, 130
proliferation, 16, 83, 90
psychological stress, 18
psychology, 33, 87
public domain, 118
public policy, 11

Q

qualifications, 12, 82, 116
quality assurance, 104, 109, 113
quality control, 127
questioning, 55
quizzes, 85

R

race, 32
radio, 2, 9, 71, 79, 94
range, 3, 4, 7, 19, 24, 25, 33, 34, 37, 84, 92, 98, 99, 106, 109, 119, 125, 127, 129, 132, 134
reading, 10, 18, 42, 95
reality, 23, 33, 36, 40, 44, 47, 48, 55, 60, 71, 75, 77, 98, 108, 115, 128, 137
reasoning, 15, 36
reasoning skills, 15
recall, 85
recognition, 111, 115
reconstruction, 98
recreation, 55
recruiting, 103, 113
redistribution, 119
reflection, 60, 85
reforms, 78, 116
regulation, 84, 113
regulations, 82, 117
reinforcement, 108, 118
relationship, 18, 19
relationships, 18, 27
relevance, 57, 64
remediation, 23, 132
replication, 118
reputation, 79, 90, 92
research funding, 113
resistance, 20, 49, 53, 125
resources, 10, 13, 23, 26, 31, 39, 43, 44, 50, 58, 61, 70, 75, 77, 91, 92, 93, 94, 95, 98, 100, 105, 109, 112, 113, 121, 132, 136
restructuring, 15, 64, 96, 116
revenue, 26, 103, 111, 114
rewards, 23, 24, 115
rhetoric, 40, 71
rhythm, 85
risk, 114
Romania, 71
Ross M. G., 17
Rothblatt S., 18
Rowntree D., 21, 132
rural population, 74

S

Samoa, 152
sample, 10, 40
satellite, 94, 127
savings, 67, 85
scarce resources, 113, 115
scattering, 26
scholarship, 60, 124
school, 8, 11, 12, 50, 58, 71, 81, 88, 108, 110, 136
school enrollment, 88
scores, 27, 42, 136
search, 59
searches, 25
second language, 136
Second World, 19
secondary education, 41, 70
secondary schools, 116
security, 88, 106
self-confidence, 115
self-efficacy, 27
self-esteem, 27
self-paced learning, 124
self-study, 22, 38, 79, 94
sensing, 89

separation, 8, 9
Septem Artes Liberales, 17
September 11, 81
series, 19
Sewart D., 18, 19
shape, 89, 117, 135
shaping, 18, 28, 80, 83, 84, 131
sharing, 60, 62, 67, 119, 121
shores, 105
signs, 28, 90
simulation, 98, 137
Singapore, 73, 74
skills, 13, 15, 22, 36, 42, 48, 55, 57, 59, 61, 87, 96, 97, 99, 132
social acceptance, 79
social class, 11
social construct, 61
social justice, 113
social learning, 50
socialization, 132
Socrates, 109
software, 1, 3, 10, 36, 65, 67, 119, 120
software code, 120
South Africa, 70, 74, 137, 162, 164
Spain, 9, 79
specialization, 132
species, 21, 55
spectrum, 1, 61, 73, 137
speed, 126, 133
stability, 106, 107
staff development, 40
staffing, 25
stages, 8, 10, 19, 77, 129
standardization, 21, 22, 67, 127
standards, 20, 67, 113
statistics, 96
steel, 66, 72, 109
storage, 33, 119
strategies, 10, 23, 40, 64, 69, 70, 81, 90, 114, 132
stress, 27, 35, 36, 56, 98, 134
stretching, 39, 44
student achievement, 37, 41, 42
student enrollment, 103
student motivation, 31
students, 3, 4, 5, 6, 7, 8, 9, 10, 11, 12, 13, 15, 16, 17, 18, 19, 20, 22, 23, 25, 26, 27, 28, 31, 32, 33, 34, 35, 38, 39, 41, 42, 43, 44, 47, 48, 49, 50, 51, 52, 53, 54, 55, 56, 57, 58, 59, 61, 63, 64, 65, 71, 72, 75, 80, 81, 82, 83, 84, 87, 90, 91, 92, 93, 94, 95, 97, 99, 102, 103, 104, 106, 107, 108, 109, 110, 111, 112, 113, 116, 118, 119, 124, 126, 127, 128, 129, 130, 134, 135, 136, 137
substitution, 7
summer, 8, 108
Sun, 105, 138, 164
supervision, 8
supply, 38
support staff, 24, 74, 129
Supreme Court, 72
surprise, 94, 126
sustainability, 76
Sweden, 125
switching, 21
Switzerland, 9, 74
symptoms, 27
systems, 4, 5, 7, 10, 15, 28, 36, 39, 54, 64, 65, 69, 71, 75, 76, 78, 81, 82, 83, 89, 94, 98, 101, 102, 104, 106, 107, 108, 109, 116, 124, 125, 126, 129, 131, 137

T

target population, 8, 11, 52, 92
teachers, 4, 5, 6, 8, 9, 16, 19, 20, 22, 23, 24, 25, 32, 33, 34, 36, 41, 49, 56, 60, 61, 65, 88, 93, 100, 129, 132, 133, 135, 138
teaching, 2, 3, 4, 5, 7, 9, 10, 11, 13, 15, 16, 17, 18, 19, 20, 21, 22, 23, 24, 25, 27, 28, 29, 30, 31, 34, 35, 36, 37, 38, 39, 40, 41, 42, 43, 44, 47, 48, 49, 51, 52, 53, 57, 59, 61, 63, 65, 66, 70, 72, 74, 78, 79, 87, 88, 89, 91, 92, 93, 94, 95, 96, 97, 99, 100, 102, 107, 108, 114, 115, 118, 119, 120, 121, 124, 126, 129, 130, 131, 132, 133, 135, 136
teaching effectiveness, 27

teaching/learning activities, 30
teaching/learning process, 3, 10, 52, 91, 108
technological advancement, 98
technological change, 73
technological developments, 134
technology, 2, 4, 9, 13, 15, 22, 24, 25, 26, 28, 35, 36, 38, 39, 41, 43, 48, 53, 54, 55, 57, 60, 63, 66, 75, 77, 79, 87, 97, 98, 99, 100, 101, 105, 110, 116, 119, 123, 129, 135, 137
telecommunications, 88
teleconferencing, 6, 9, 127
telephone, 6, 137
television, 6, 9, 21, 71, 79, 132
tertiary education, 9, 20, 62, 70, 135
textbooks, 4, 38, 95
Thailand, 9
theory, 21, 35, 60, 61, 93
think critically, 57
thinking, 15, 32, 98
Tight M., 18
time, 6, 8, 9, 12, 15, 20, 22, 24, 25, 27, 29, 31, 32, 34, 38, 47, 49, 50, 52, 53, 54, 57, 58, 60, 63, 72, 81, 83, 85, 88, 91, 95, 96, 97, 107, 113, 116, 117, 118, 128, 129, 132, 133, 134, 135, 136, 138
top-down decisions, 115
trade, 1, 80, 87, 107, 109
trademarks, 117
trade-off, 87
trading, 116
trading bloc, 116
tradition, 18, 21, 83
traffic, 120
training, 15, 16, 25, 26, 28, 41, 44, 52, 54, 57, 62, 64, 70, 72, 80, 85, 86, 89, 92, 107, 108, 112, 124, 137
training programs, 64, 85, 89, 92
transformation, 15, 135
transition, 112
transmission, 3, 79, 123, 131
transparency, 82
trend, 48, 52, 80, 81, 98, 102, 113, 115, 116, 117, 127, 130
trust, 27, 115
Turkey, 146
tutoring, 48, 58

U

uncertainty, 28
UNESCO, 2, 37, 52, 70, 74, 75, 83, 104, 121, 125, 141, 148, 149, 152, 158, 163, 164
unit cost, 99
United Kingdom (UK), 9, 24, 30, 39, 63, 73, 74, 78, 79, 80, 81, 102, 108, 109, 110, 112, 148, 155, 164
United States, 139, 144, 147, 162
universities, 1, 3, 4, 5, 7, 8, 10, 11, 12, 15, 17, 18, 19, 21, 22, 28, 36, 38, 39, 40, 48, 49, 50, 51, 52, 59, 62, 63, 64, 66, 71, 72, 73, 75, 78, 79, 80, 81, 82, 83, 84, 85, 86, 87, 88, 89, 90, 91, 92, 93, 94, 95, 96, 101, 102, 104, 105, 106, 107, 109, 110, 111, 112, 113, 114, 116, 117, 120, 124, 125, 126, 129, 130, 131, 134, 135, 137
university education, 30, 75
University of Bologna, 17
university students, 15
updating, 95, 96, 97
urban areas, 12
US Department of Commerce, 80

V

values, 27, 31, 32, 85
variables, 69
venture capital, 3
vice-president, 115
video games, 138
Vietnam, 125
village, 73
virtual university, 4
visas, 81
vision, 16, 36, 54, 55
vocabulary, 80

voice, 137
Volkswagen, 86

W

watershed, 72
wealth, 6, 69
web, 2, 4, 5, 6, 13, 37, 56, 112
Western Europe, 120
windows, 88
women, 12, 74
word processing, 10, 39
workers, 64, 87, 128
working conditions, 22
workload, 23, 27
workplace, 27
World Bank, 40, 70, 71, 74, 75, 76, 77, 95, 121, 145, 160, 163, 165, 166
World War I, 102, 164
World Wide Web, 31, 35, 102, 108, 110, 164
worry, 119
writing, 29, 32

Y

yield, 42, 64, 114

Z

Zittle R., 21, 132